高职高专旅游类专业精品教材

酒店实用英语
灵活运用篇

ENGLISH FOR HOTEL STAFF-DEVELOPING SKILLS

张 茵 主编　周雅菊 副主编

清华大学出版社
北京

内 容 简 介

本教材主要培养酒店、旅游专业学生或酒店服务人员的英语听说能力以及在实际工作岗位上的英语运用能力，突出行业外语的应用能力培养。本书内容还原了工作本来面貌，注重以实际工作流程为导向，同时紧扣《酒店运营管理职业技能等级证书》。本系列教材贯彻党的二十大精神，内容融入中国特色的思政元素。书中内容不仅与职业资格证书挂钩与行业接轨，实现分层次培养人才的目的，而且密切结合酒店前厅、客房、餐饮等岗位群的典型工作任务，突出现代旅游服务业从业人员的英语语言表达、人际交往与沟通协调能力及应变能力的综合素质的培养。

感谢常州新城希尔顿酒店和江苏凤凰台饭店集团有限公司的大力支持，本书图片由其授权许可使用。
本书封面贴有清华大学出版社防伪标签，无标签者不得销售。
版权所有，侵权必究。举报：010-62782989，beiqinquan@tup.tsinghua.edu.cn。

图书在版编目（CIP）数据

酒店实用英语. 灵活运用篇 / 张茵主编. — 北京：清华大学出版社，2017（2024.8重印）
（高职高专旅游类专业精品教材）
ISBN 978-7-302-47339-8

Ⅰ. ①酒⋯　Ⅱ. ①张⋯　Ⅲ. ①饭店 – 英语 – 高等职业教育 – 教材　Ⅳ. ① F719.3

中国版本图书馆 CIP 数据核字（2017）第 124099 号

责任编辑：王如月　周　菁
封面设计：常雪影
责任校对：王凤芝
责任印制：杨　艳

出版发行：清华大学出版社
网　　址：https://www.tup.com.cn，https://www.wqxuetang.com
地　　址：北京清华大学学研大厦A座　　　　邮　编：100084
社 总 机：010-83470000　　　　　　　　　　邮　购：010-62786544
投稿与读者服务：010-62776969，c-service@tup.tsinghua.edu.cn
质量反馈：010-62772015，zhiliang@tup.tsinghua.edu.cn
印 装 者：涿州市般润文化传播有限公司
经　　销：全国新华书店
开　　本：210mm×285mm　　印　张：15.25　　字　数：274千字
版　　次：2017年12月第1版　　　　　　　　印　次：2024年8月第4次印刷
定　　价：99.00元

产品编号：062479-02

本书编委会

主　编：张　茵

副主编：周雅菊

成　员（以姓氏拼音为序）

　　　　是　静　宋长来　陶玉婷　王　玲　王贺玲　吴　敏

　　　　辛衍君　徐　沁　徐　岩　颜　君　尹　奎　张秀芹

　　　　郑国中　周　丽

前 言

中国作为世界旅游板块的亚太核心,正在发挥越来越重要的作用。《中华人民共和国国民经济和社会发展第十四个五年规划和2035年远景目标纲要》中有多处提到旅游产业发展,包括"加快发展健康、养老、托育、文化、旅游、体育、物业等服务业""推动购物消费、居家生活、旅游休闲、交通出行等各类场景数字化,打造智慧共享、和睦共治的新型数字生活""深入发展大众旅游、智慧旅游,创新旅游产品体系,改善旅游消费体验""推动文化和旅游融合发展"等,足见政府对旅游业升级发展的持续关注。党的二十大报告中提及的"坚持以文塑旅、以旅彰文,推进文化和旅游深度融合发展","深入实施科教兴国战略、人才强国战略、创新驱动发展战略"等,坚持为党育人、为国育才,体现了未来旅游市场的广阔前景以及对行业人才的高标准要求。

随着中国文化自信、中国文化走出去,旅游业作为开放性、综合性产业,在共建"一带一路"战略中发挥着独特优势。现代旅游服务行业的岗位对旅游从业人员的对外服务能力提出了更高的要求。《教育部关于加强高职高专教育人才培养工作的意见》中明确提出:高职高专教育"以适应社会需要为目标、以培养技术应用能力为主线设计学生的知识、能力、素质结构和培养方案,毕业生应具有基础理论知识适度、技术应用能力强、知识面较宽、素质高等特点""课程和教学内容体系改革是高职高专教学改革的重点和难点"。

《酒店实用英语(基础会话篇)》和《酒店实用英语(灵活运用篇)》是站在国家职业教育与人才培养的战略高度,密切结合国家人才培养的价值引领和高校课程思政建设的战略意义,响应"一带一路"国家战略需要,结合高职教育的国内外优秀专业师资(同时具有教学经验与行业经验)、行业专家的指导意见与行业标准、精心打造出版的一系列通用酒店服务行业英语教材。

一、教材特色

本套教材主要有以下特色:

巧妙融入课程思政,信息时代"活学活用"。本教材在编写过程中与时俱进,教学内容融入中国特色的思政元素,培养学生语用理解和表达能力,提高文化语境意识,培养学生的"家国情怀"和"世界眼光";补充现代酒店服务的新流程,包括目前流行的网络预订、快捷支付、机器人送餐等环节。书中每个模块都有一个二维码,读者直接扫描就可以在移动终端上收听相关的音频和对话信息,随时随地学习、掌握。

PREFACE

以行业证书为标准，满足不同学生实际需要。本教材依据《国家餐饮服务师职业资格考试》《国家客房服务师资格考试》和《酒店运营管理职业技能等级证书》中关于英语语言的使用标准和要求，设计内容和难度，分为基础会话和灵活运用两个部分。该教材以职业活动为导向，建立以职业功能为主线、主题情境为载体工作任务为驱动的学习方式，结合职业资格证书（技能证书）制度与高职学历教育的有机结合即"融通"，满足不同水平学生的实际需求。

还原工作本来面貌，以实际工作流程为导向。本教材依据真实职业岗位工作流程精心设计主题情境，教材内容与职业标准对接，每个主题情境下设若干具体的小任务。教材设计以酒店各部门工作场所为载体，两个级别共包括 12 个模块、40 个主题学习情境和 120 个工作任务，基本上涵盖了酒店服务的各个环节。通过细化工作任务，确保教学内容真实有效，提高教学内容针对性及职业岗位能力培养适用性。侧重选择过程完整、相对独立的工作任务，使学生在完成任务的过程中形成解决实际问题的能力。

二、教材结构

以《酒店实用英语（基础会话篇）》为例，全书共有 6 个模块，20 个主题情境，60 个子任务。课文所有学习内容均以完成任务、解决问题入手，侧重听说训练及课堂小组讨论，没有堆砌大量对话。对话文本在附录中体现，更侧重知识的实际运用性、趣味性和可操作性。整本教材结构如下：

（1）全书以酒店实际工作内容来设计教学内容，分为酒店概述、前厅服务、客房服务、餐饮服务、商务中心服务、特殊服务 6 个模块。

（2）每个模块分别设置不同的主题情境，每个主题情境都设有任务目标，其目的是使教师和学生能在任务开始前掌握本情境的教学重点。

（3）Introduction：每个主题情境通过其部门功能介绍引入学习任务，其目的是使教师和学生对该部门工作职能再次加深了解。

（4）Brainstorm：头脑风暴，通过讨论回忆并总结基础会话部分所学过并掌握的词汇及表达，为本模块知识的引入和掌握起到铺垫作用。

（5）Tasks：每个主题情境根据具体职业要求分为 3~4 个子任务，学习内容从解决问题入手，总结子任务中常见短语和句子表达，随即进行有针对性的练习，便于学生迅速掌握相关知识和技能。

（6）Vocabulary：提供酒店场景对话中常用的英语词汇，便于学生校音记忆。

前言

（7）Exercise：提供实务场景资料，通过翻译、口译、讨论、阅读等练习，帮助学生更有效地掌握语言运用及职业技能。

（8）Tips：提供相关语言使用贴士或者行业小短文，开阔视野，供学有余力的学生使用。

（9）Dialogue-Scripts：展示本书所有主题情境对话原稿，帮助学生课前预习或课后复习总结。

（10）Appendix：附录部分提供补充资料，包括酒店管理人员岗位名称、餐饮常用词汇，方便学生学习和工作中查询使用。

三、教材使用说明

本套教材的主编根据其多年教研经验和在酒店一线工作的经历，结合自己在加拿大和美国访学期间阅读的大量外版书，在教材内容的设计上鼓励学生探讨式学习、注重培养学生的思维创新能力。教材编写者均为长期从事酒店经营管理专业教学并具有一线经验的专业教师：第一、三部分及附录由常州工业职业技术学院的张茵老师编写，第二、四、五、六部分由常州工业职业技术学院的周雅菊老师编写。

书中我们还专门为授课教师提供了《酒店服务英语教学参考大纲》，教师可参考大纲内的课时数安排进行教学、也可根据教学实际情况进行课时数的调整。此外，每册教材均配有教学课件和二维码扫码收听语音功能，方便教师授课使用。本系列教材既适合高职高专酒店管理专业学生学习使用，也可作为酒店行业培训教材和酒店从业人员的自学教材。本教材为全英文教材，也适用于"一带一路"留学生酒店管理专业的课程教学。

教材成稿之后，我们还广泛听取了国内外酒店英语教育专家和国际酒店业高管的意见和建议。教材的编写凝聚了诸多专家学者的经验和智慧。在此，对为本套教材的编写和出版付出辛勤劳动的所有老师、行业专家及出版社的各位老师表示衷心的感谢。特别要感谢常州新城希尔顿酒店的大力支持。由于编写能力和编写时间有限，疏漏之处在所难免，恳请广大读者和专家批评指正。

编者写于2023年夏

酒店服务英语教学参考大纲
（灵活运用篇）

（课时建议：42学时，注重服务的种类和多样性及英语语言表达的准确性）

序号	学习情境	工作任务	学时
模块一	**The Front Desk 前厅服务英语**		**10课时**
1-1	Room Reservations 预订服务	FIT Reservation, Group Reservation, Reservation Revision, Over-booking 个人预订，团队预订，预订变更，超额预订	2
1-2	At the Reception Desk 接待服务	Early Check-in, Extending the Stay, Changing the Room 提前入住，办理续住，更换房间	2
1-3	Business Center 商务中心服务	Ticket Booking, Renting Equipment, Interpretation Service 票务服务，租借设备，翻译服务	2
1-4	Concierge Service 礼宾服务	Pick-up Service, Luggage Deposit, Mail Delivery 接机服务，行李寄存，快件处理	2
1-5	The Cashier 收银服务	Credit Card Payment, Cash Payment, Foreign Currency Exchange 信用卡结账，现金结账，外币兑换	2
模块二	**Housekeeping Department 客房服务英语**		**6课时**
2-1	Chamber Service 客房服务	Cleaning the Room, Turn-down Service, Adding Beds 清扫客房，做晚床，加床服务	2
2-2	Laundry Service 洗衣服务	Express Service, Special Requirements, Laundry Damage 快洗服务，特殊要求，洗衣损坏	2
2-3	Personal Service 个性服务	Wake-up Service, Shoe-shining Service, Baby-sitting Service, Maintenance Service 叫醒服务，擦鞋服务，托婴服务，维修服务	2
模块三	**Food & Beverage Department 餐饮服务英语**		**10课时**
3-1	Welcoming Guests 迎客服务	Serving Reserved Guests, Serving Non-reserved Guests, Changing the Table 接待已预订客人，接待未预订客人，更换餐桌	2
3-2	Taking Orders 点菜服务	Western food, Chinese food, Buffet 西餐，中餐，自助餐	2

序号	学习情境	工 作 任 务	学时
3-3	Serving Dishes 上菜服务	Slow in Serving, Serving Wrong Dish, Special Service 上菜慢，上错菜，特殊服务	2
3-4	Bar Service 酒吧服务	Serving Wines, Communicating with Guests, Conflict Resolution 酒水服务，与客交谈，处理状况	2
3-5	Room Service 客房送餐服务	Doorknob Menu, Ordering Meals, Serving Meals 门把菜单，电话点餐，送餐服务	2
模块四	**Other Services　其他服务英语**		6课时
4-1	Conference Services 会议服务	Introduction of Facilities, Contract Negotiation, Conference Registration 设施介绍，合同商谈，会议签到	2
4-2	Recreation Services 康乐服务	Fitness Center, Beauty Salon, Massage Center 健身服务，美容美发服务，按摩服务	2
4-3	Shopping Arcade 商场服务	Choosing a Gift, Chinese Porcelain, Chinese Painting 礼物推荐，购买中国瓷器，购买中国画	2
模块五	**Emergencies & Complaints　应急和投诉处理**		4课时
5-1	Handling Emergencies 处理紧急情况	Asking For a Doctor, Elevator Emergency, Fire Emergency 寻找医生，电梯事故，火灾	2
5-2	Settling Complaints 处理投诉	Settling Complaints about Reservation, Settling Complaints about Room Facilities, Settling Complaints about Food 订房投诉，客房投诉，餐厅投诉	2
模块六	**Hotel Management & Orientation　酒店管理与求职**		4课时
6-1	Hotel Management 酒店管理	Promotion, Interviews & Orientation 酒店推销，面试和迎新	2
6-2	Career and Resume 职业简历	Career Advice, Resume Templates 职业建议，简历模板	2

目 录

Part 1 The Front Desk
前厅服务英语   1

Scene One	Room Reservations	2
Scene Two	At the Reception Desk	9
Scene Three	Business Center	15
Scene Four	Concierge Service	23
Scene Five	The Cashier	30

Part 2 Housekeeping Department
客房服务英语   39

Scene One	Chamber Service	40
Scene Two	Laundry Service	47
Scene Three	Personal Service	53

Part 3 Food & Beverage Department
餐饮服务英语   61

Scene One	Welcoming Guests	62
Scene Two	Taking Orders	68
Scene Three	Serving Dishes	75
Scene Four	Bar Service	82
Scene Five	Room Service	89

CONTENTS

Part 4 Other Services 其他服务英语   97

Scene One	Conference Services	98
Scene Two	Recreation Services	104
Scene Three	Shopping Arcade	110

Part 5 Emergencies & Complaints 应急和投诉处理   117

Scene One	Handling Emergencies	118
Scene Two	Settling Complaints	124

Part 6 Hotel Management & Orientation 酒店管理与求职   131

Scene One	Hotel Management	132
Scene Two	Career and Resume	138

目 录

Appendix Ⅰ: Traditional Festivals   226
Appendix Ⅱ: Housekeeping Vocabulary   227
Appendix Ⅲ: Tableware   228
Appendix Ⅳ: Food   230
参考文献   231

The Front Desk
前厅服务英语

Part 1

Brainstorm

Please look at the picture of the Front Desk in this hotel, and describe what features this Front Desk presents. As a class, list the words that describe the possible staff, services, amenities or facilities this hotel may provide. Then discuss them with your groups. See which group has the most extensive vocabulary.

people, places, things, services…

Scene One — Room Reservations

The Reservation Desk should promptly and enthusiastically handle all telephone reservation inquires and requests. And with efficiency and accuracy process all reservations, in accordance with the established standards and procedures, ensuring consistent customer satisfaction and maximum revenues for the Hotel. In addition, the Reservation Desk must maintain a good working relationship with all other departments within the Hotel providing well maintained occupancy forecasts, reports and statistical data. Well-polished telephone skills and sales abilities of the Reservations staff play a vital role in forming positive perceptions of the Hotel and its parent-company. It also serves potential clients while reinforcing the Hotel's reputation for high standards and those loyal clients.

In this unit, you will learn:

FIT Reservation

Group Reservation

Reservation Revision

Over-booking

Activities

FIT Reservation

Listen to the dialogue about FIT Reservation and fill in the reservation slip below.

DEMO. COPY		For Registration Call 0519-****-****
RESERVATION SLIP		
Reservation # 1		Enquiry Date: 05 / 26 / 20** (Month) (Date) (Year)
Arrival Date:		Departure Date:
Guest's Name:		
Room # 203		
Floor: 2nd Floor		Facilities:
Room Type:		
No. of Beds:		
Prepared by:	Manager:	Enquirer:

Useful Expressions

Good morning, Shangri-la Hotel. **May I help you**?

Would you like to have a single room or a double room?

Let me check …yes, we have a single room **available**.

It's easy to …

A single room is RMB … yuan per night.

What time will you be arriving?

May I have your name and contact number, please?

Would you please spell your name?

We are looking forward to your arriving.

Practice:

Please look at the following poster online from Hilton Ft. Lauderdale Hotel by the beach. Work in pairs and take turns role-playing the Reservation staff and the potential guest. The guest plans to visit the city alone and stay for several days. Try to use the sentences learned in the recording.

Group Reservation

Listen to the dialogue about group reservation and answer the following questions:

a. What's the name of the visiting group?
b. How many guests in the group? When will they arrive and depart?
c. What type of rooms do they prefer? What type of rooms did they have in the end?
d. Is there any special rate for this group reservation?
e. Who will be responsible for all of the hotel expenses? And how do they plan to pay?

Useful Expressions

May I know how many people in your group for this conference?
I'm afraid that we can only confirm 2 single rooms with double beds, **but** we have more twin rooms with rear views for those days.
There will be a 12 percent discount.
You should pay a deposit of RMB 1200 yuan.
How do you plan to settle the accounts, please?
Is there anything else I can do for you?

Practice:

Are there any differences between the F.I.T. Reservation and the Group Reservation?

Reservation Revision

Listen to a few short conversations of people asking for reservation revisions at Holiday Inn. Please complete the conversations by filling in the missing words and expressions as you listen to the dialogues.

A. The guest "May" made a room reservation for 3 nights. She wants to extend her stay for 5 nights. The hotel clerk helps her to revise the reservation.

(C=Clerk, M=May)

C: _____. May I please help you?

M: Good afternoon. My name is May, and I have made a reservation at Holiday Inn _____. I'd like to extend my stay here for 2 more nights until the 12th.

C: _____?

M: That's right.

C: Is there any change in your _____? You reserved a double room with a double bed.

M: No.

C: Thank you, madam. _____.

B. **Marisa, an agent from Youth Travel Agency, has booked 15 rooms in Sunrise Hotel in the name of the agency. But due to a revised travel schedule, she is calling the hotel to alter the reservation. (C=Clerk, M=Marisa)**

C: Good morning. Sunrise Hotel. _____?

M: Yes. This is Marisa calling from Canada. I have to change the arrival date of my reservation.

C: Ok. _____?

M: Yes. It's under the name of the company "Youth Travel Agency".

C: Ok. Let me check …you've booked _____ for September 15th to 17th, right?

M: Right. And is it possible for us to postpone the arrival dates from September 21st to 23rd?

C: Please wait for a minute, let me check …yes, _____.

M: That's perfect!

C: So, you have changed your booking of 15 twin rooms from September 21st to 23rd, under the name of "Youth Travel Agency", is that correct?

M: Yes, it is. Thanks a lot!

C: _____. Have a nice day!

Useful Expressions

Would you please tell me under whose name has the reservation been made?
How would you like to change, sir?
Is there any change in your room type?
How long do you plan to stay?
Please wait for a minute, **let me** check …
Yes, **we have** enough twin rooms available for those days.
We will extend the reservation for you.

Practice:

Suppose you are a reservationist working in Marriot Hotel in Beijing. In the morning, you receive an email from Robert, a guest in your hotel. Make a dialogue on reservation revision according to the content below.

> Subject: Re: Smart Study Tour
> Dear Sir,
> We regret to inform you that the above mentioned group will not be coming to Beijing this October 7th, as originally planned. We understand that the group will be traveling to Beijing in this December 6th. Would you please help us to change the reservation date from October 7th to December 6th? The room type will be still 6 double rooms and 1 suite. Looking forward to your reply. Thank you!
>
> Sincerely yours,
> Stevan

Over-booking

Listen to the following dialogue and complete the conversation. Pay attention to the sentences used by the reservationist about how to refuse the reservation politely.

Alice is calling New Asian Hotel to reserve a double room. The reservation clerk is answering the phone.

Clerk: Good morning, New Asian Hotel. Reservations. May I help you?
Alice: I'd like to book a triple room for June 13th.
Clerk: Just a moment, please …sorry, _____. You know it is the popular season for the seaside summer festival here. Is it possible for you _____?
Alice: Oh, no. We will come to attend a very important conference in another hotel nearby. And that hotel has been fully booked already. That's a great pity!
Clerk: I'm very sorry. _____.
Alice: That's very kind of you. But could you recommend another hotel nearby to me?
Clerk: In this case, I would suggest that you try Green Forest Inn. They usually have a large number of triple rooms for the young people who have package tours here. The telephone number is _____.
Alice: Thank you so much. I really appreciate your help!
Clerk: _____. Goodbye!

Useful Expressions

I'm afraid our hotel is fully booked for that day.
Is it possible for you to change the arrival date?
I will **put** you **on** our waiting list and call you if there is a cancellation.
In this case, I would **suggest** that you try Green Forest Inn.
Thank you for calling us.

Practice:

There is usually a heavy demand for all the hotel rooms during the peak seasons and it is very difficult for the guests to make a reservation during this period. Please discuss the Source of Room Demand in Alberta with your classmates and try to conclude what are the main sources and the possible reasons.

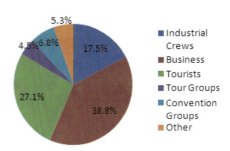

Vocabulary

accordance	[ə'kɔ:dns]	n.	一致，和谐
account	[ə'kaʊnt]	n.	账目，存款
agency	['eɪdʒənsi]	n.	代理，机构
appreciate	[ə'pri:ʃieɪt]	v.	感激，感谢，欣赏
conference	['kɒnfərəns]	v.	会议
confirm	[kən'fɜ:m]	v.	证实，确认
deposit	[dɪ'pɒzɪt]	n.	保证金，押金，寄存；
		v.	寄存
discount	['dɪskaʊnt]	n.	折扣额；
		v.	打折
enquiry	[ɪn'kwaɪərɪ]	n.	询问，问讯处
expense	[ɪk'spens]	n.	费用，花费的钱
extend	[ɪk'stend]	v.	表达，给予
facility	[fə'sɪləti]	n.	设备
postpone	[pəʊs'pəʊn]	v.	使延期，延缓
revision	[rɪ'vɪʒn]	n.	修订，修改

FIT (foreign Individual Tourist) 　　国外散客，个人旅游者
over-booking 　　超额预订
package tour 　　包价旅游，包办旅游
rear view 　　后面景色，背面景色
12 percent discount 　　打七八折，12%的折扣

Exercises

I. Please translate the following sentences:
1. 请问您是要单人间还是双人间呢?
2. 请问你们参加会议的一共多少人?
3. 这个月我们酒店有20%的折扣。
4. 您将如何结算这笔费用呢?
5. 我会把您列入我们的候房名单。如果有人取消预订,我会打电话给您。
6. Let me check … yes, we have a single room available.
7. Is it possible for you to change the arrival date?
8. A single room is RMB 698 yuan per night.
9. You will have to pay a deposit of RMB 1200 yuan.
10. I'm afraid our hotel is fully booked for that day.

II. Role-play: Work in groups of two. Use the information below with your group members and try to make up dialogues about FIT Reservation or Group Reservation.

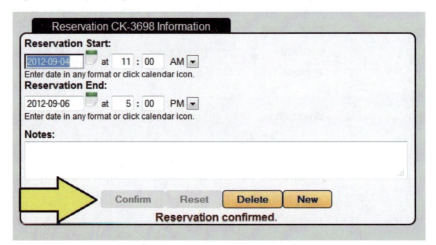

III. Please look at the following picture and discuss how to make a reservation online. Then put each step in the correct order.

A. The guest presents the voucher to the hotel. (   )
B. Reservation agent will send Quotation/Price for the room reservation (Rooms not yet confirmed). (   )
C. The guest pays for the room reservation. (   )
D. The guest will receive Autoresponder Email/Acknowledgement that reservation request has been received. (   )
E. Once reservation agent receives a confirmation form from guest through email, reservation agent will confirm room availability and send details for payment. (   )
F. The guest will send reservation request (fill up the reservation form). (   )
G. The guest must email to confirm if the price is acceptable and check reservation details if it is correct. (   )
H. Once payment is done, reservation agent will send reservation voucher to the guest. (   )

How to Make the Reservation Revision or Cancellation?

Sometimes a guest may change his/her planned visit and may request for a revision or cancellation of the reservation. The following steps should be followed up during the revision or cancellation of reservation:

Take down the necessary details on the reservation revision/cancellation form.

Update the reservation chart by removing the room allocation made from the earlier dates. Allocate the rooms on the new dates in case of revision.

Remove the reservation slip from the reservation rack. In case of revision, make a new reservation slip including two copies. Attach one with the reservation revision/cancellation form and keep another copy in the reservation rack in alphabetical order.

Scene Two — At the Reception Desk

The reception desk is the first place visitors see when entering a hotel and it's also the location where guests are greeted. The hotel reception staff should make guests feel welcome, manage room bookings and deal with requests that guests make during their stay. The hotel reception staff also needs to be friendly and professional at all times with a well-groomed appearance. To qualify for this position, an individual needs to have a good background in general education, specialized professional skills such as English, math and IT. They also need experience using a telephone switchboard or a computerized reservation system. Being away from home and tired from traveling, a guest wants to feel welcome and to have a peaceful rest in his room quickly. So reception staff should try their best to create a home away from home for their guests as much as possible.

In this unit, you will learn:

Early Check-in

Extending the Stay

Changing the Room

Activities

Early Check-in

Please listen to the dialogue and answer the following questions.

a. When did the guest reserve online?
b. What kind of room does the guest want and how long will he stay in the hotel?
c. What time is the standard check-in time?
d. Why is immediate check-in impossible for the guest?
e. What two things does the receptionist suggest to the guest?
f. How can you find the Lobby Lounge?

Useful Expressions

You are staying with us for 2 nights, **right**?

I'm sorry, Mr Tom Brown. Your room **isn't quite ready** yet.

Normally our check-in begins at 3 p.m.

I'm sorry but Housekeeping are **still** cleaning your room now.

You **are welcome to** store your luggage with us.

May I **suggest** you have a cup of coffee and relax in our Lobby Lounge?

I'll ask Housekeeping to do your room **as quickly as possible**.

Practice:

Please discuss with your partner and practice how to apologize to your guests. Try to use "*I'm sorry …*", "*I apologize that …*", "*I am afraid …*"

a. Your room isn't ready yet, madam.

b. You are too early for check in, sir.

c. Housekeeping staff is still cleaning the rooms, sir.

d. We don't have any rooms ready at the moment.

Extending The Stay

Listen to the dialogue and try to create a new record in the computer.

Dalian Seaside Beach Hotel	Dalian Seaside Beach Hotel
Guest's Name: *Susan Miller*	Guest's Name: Susan Miller
Room Number: *3832 3834*	Room Number: _____
Check-in Date: *Aug. 4*	Check-in Date: Aug. 4
Check-out Date: *Aug.6*	Check-out Date: _____
Rate: *870 yuan*	Rate: _____
Room Type: *Double room*	Room Type: _____
Bed: *queen bed*	Bed: _____

Useful Expressions

Let me **check it** in the computer.

One of your two rooms **has been registered** by a business group for tonight.

Would you **mind transferring** to the room 3660?

By the way, the rate is 200 yuan **higher because** it's a business room with a king bed instead of the queen bed.

The guest in this room will check out at 11:00 a.m. and I will **inform** you then.

Practice:

Now please discuss with your classmates and write down the service procedures for extending the stay in your hotel.

Changing the Room

Please complete the conversation by filling in the missing words and expressions.

(R=Receptionist, G=Guest)

R: Good morning, madam. _____ for you?

G: Yes. I'd like to change my room.

R: Is there anything specifically wrong with your room?

G: I want to change my room to a quieter one, because _____. The room I'm staying in is near _____ and it's so _____ at night. More than that, it smells like _____.

R: I'm very sorry to hear that, madam. Some guests unfortunately ignore the Non-smoking signs. May I know your name and your room number?

G: Sally Taylor from room _____.

R: Ok, Ms Taylor. Do you want the same type of room?

G: Yes, _____ room with _____ bed, please.

R: I see. Please wait for a moment, I will check the computer for you. There is a single room on the _____ floor and it's _____. The room rate is same. would you want this one?

G: Yes, I will take it.

R: The room number is 1349. Would you please fill in this _____?

G: Sure. Here it is. And this is my room card.

R: Thank you, madam. Here is your new room card. You can come to your new room right away.

G: It's very kind of you. Thank you.

R: My pleasure. _____.

Useful Expressions

Is there **anything specifically wrong with** your room?

Some guests unfortunately **ignore** the Non-smoking signs.

Please wait for a moment. I will check the computer **for you**.

Do you want **the same type** of room?

Would you please fill in this **room-change form**?

Here is your new room card and you can go to your new room **right away**.

Practice:

Now please discuss with your classmates and put the following service steps in the right order.

Ask the guest to fill in the room changing form. _____
Check the computer record to find the room availability. _____
Greet the guest. _____
If there is a room available, change the room for the guest and make a record of the changing information. ____4____
Confirm the guest about room changing details including name, time, room type and room number. _____
Get to know the guest's room number. _____
Extend your best wishes. _____

Vocabulary

change	[tʃeɪndʒ]	n.	零钱；
		v.	变更，兑换
corner	[ˈkɔːnə(r)]	n.	拐角，角落
entrance	[ˈentrəns]	n.	入口
ignore	[ɪɡˈnɔː(r)]	v.	忽视
inform	[ɪnˈfɔːm]	v.	通知
lounge	[laʊndʒ]	n.	休息厅，客厅
noisy	[ˈnɔɪzi]	adj.	嘈杂的，喧闹的
normally	[ˈnɔːməli]	adj.	正常地，一般地
quiet	[ˈkwaɪət]	adj.	安静的，清静的
register	[ˈredʒɪstə(r)]	v.	登记，注册
relax	[rɪˈlæks]	v.	休息，放松
seafood	[ˈsiːfuːd]	n.	海鲜
seaside	[ˈsiːsaɪd]	n.	海滨，海边；
		v.	海边的，海滨的
sign	[saɪn]	n.	指示牌，标志牌
smoke	[sməʊk]	n.	吸烟，烟；
		v.	吸烟
transfer	[trænsˈfɜː(r)]	v.	转换，调动
unfortunately	[ʌnˈfɔːtʃənətli]	adv.	遗憾地，不幸地
as quickly as possible			尽快
fresh up			梳洗，重新恢复活力
in the name of			以……的名字
instead of			代替……
non-smoking			禁止吸烟
room-change form			换房表格
trans-ocean			越洋，跨洋

Exercises

I. **Please translate the following sentences:**

1. 很抱歉，布朗先生。您的房间还没有准备好。我们通常在下午两点办理入住。
2. 您的两个房间中，今晚有一间被旅游团登记入住了。您介意搬到4039房间吗？
3. 顺便讲一下，新的房间房价要贵300元，因为这是一间大床的双人间。
4. 我会让客房部尽快清理好您的房间。
5. 这是您的新房卡，您可以马上搬到您的新房间了。
6. I'm sorry but Housekeeping is still cleaning your room now.
7. You are welcome to store your luggage with us.
8. May I suggest you have a cup of coffee and relax in our coffee bar?
9. The guest in this room will check out at 10:00 a.m. and I will inform you then.
10. Is there anything wrong with your room?

II. **Role-play:** Sean Thomas from room 902 is coming to the reception desk. He wants to extend his stay in hotel for 2 more nights. Please make up a dialogue using to the reservation record below.

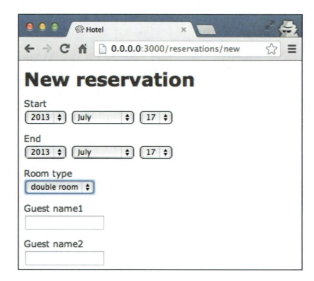

II. **Topics for Discussion**

There are many aspects of a hotel receptionist's job. In most hotels, a hotel receptionist not only provides information but also initializes the registration procedure for guests. Please discuss with your partner about the responsibilities a qualified receptionist should have.

Part 1   The Front Desk   前厅服务英语   15

Tips

How to be an excellent receptionist?

If you are a hotel receptionist working, you are the one person who will be making a first impression on almost everyone your hotel ever does business with. More than that, you are the public face of your hotel! This makes you become very important ... and if you drop the ball, your hotel may never get another chance to earn that guest's business ...

Here are several tips for hotel receptionists:

Leave your personal issues and attitude at home. You must stay focused and keep your problems to yourself. Do everything possible to deliver exceptional customer service to the guests at your hotel.

The guest may not always be right, but they are always the guest. — Your job is not to scold or correct them or even teach them a lesson.— Despite when they're at fault.— Your job is to cheerfully help them whenever they need service.

And finally, remember that words matter, so get in the habit of using the following phrases constantly, as these words can help you break down barriers and diffuse bad situations quickly. Words and phrases such as: "Thank you", "Please", "You're welcome", "My pleasure", "Good morning", "Good afternoon", "Have a great day", "Have a great weekend", etc. If you say these with a smile and a feeling of genuineness, you make your guests feel good, and you can also make yourself an excellent receptionist.

Scene Three   Business Center

Business Center provides a useful resource for hotel travelers, especially business travelers. It usually provides secretarial, translation services as well as business support including high-speed internet access, computer rentals, ground and air shipping, printing, photocopying, faxing, office supplies, business card creation, notary services, scanning, booking tickets and more.

A hotel business center clerk provides administrative support to guests. Duties may include typing, faxing and photocopying. Additionally, these individuals may educate guests on the proper use of office equipment and processes, such as computers and long-distance calling. Due to the fast-paced nature of the business, hotel business center clerks must also be energetic, excellent communicators and possess a 5-star customer-service mentality.

In this unit, you will learn:

Ticket Booking

Renting Equipment

Interpretation Service

Activities

Ticket Booking

Now you will listen to this dialogue between a clerk and a guest. Decide whether the statements are True or False.

a. The guest wants to book a train ticket from Shanghai to Sanya.
b. There are three flights available on October 9th.
c. The guest wants to take the flight at 9:50 in the morning.
d. The guest chooses the flight which will depart from Shanghai Hongqiao International Airport because it's near the hotel.

e. The guest wants a Business Class airline ticket.

f. The guest may receive the ticket in a week.

Useful Expressions

There are **three flights** available that day.

What time **is suitable for** you, morning or afternoon?

Which class would you prefer for your ticket, **economy class, business class or first class**?

And **how many** tickets do you want?

We will give you the ticket **in** two or three days.

Will you come to **pick up** your ticket or should we **send** it to your room?

Practice:

Please match the following words with their pictures.

| a. hard berth | b. soft seat | c. round trip | d. soft berth | e. first class |
| f. one way | g. hard seat | h. business class | i. economy class | |

1. _____ 2. _____ 3. _____

4. _____ 5. _____ 6. _____

7. _____ 8. _____ 9. _____

Renting Equipment

Please complete the conversation by filling in the missing words and expressions.

(C=Clerk, G=Guest)

C: Good morning, madam. Is there anything I can do for you?

G: Yes, please. I'd like to _____ tonight.

C: Certainly, madam. For how long, please?

G: _____. I need to prepare for a business report tonight.

C: No problem, madam. _____? We have a great selection of _____ laptop in the center, you see, like Levono, IBM, Toshiba or Dell. We also have _____, too.

G: Well, I need a larger size which is comfortable to use. May I have a look, please?

C: Sure. …Here they are. _____?

G: I want to rent this one, _____.

C: Great. This is a new one in good condition. Here is the rental form and the instructions. Please read the details carefully and fill in the rental form.

G: OK. So how about the charge?

C: The charge is _____ an hour. And you need to pay _____ as a deposit in advance.

G: No problem.

C: Could you show me your room card, please?

G: Here you are. By the way, is there _____ or _____ in the room? I need to work online.

C: Yes, madam. We do have free WiFi in all our rooms, and here is our _____ and _____.

G: Wonderful. Thank you for your help.

C: You are welcome, madam. Have a nice day!

Useful Expressions

Which **brand** do you prefer?

We have a **great selection of** laptops in the center.

Here is the rental form and the **instructions**.

Please **read** the details carefully and **fill** in the form.

The charge is 15 yuan **an hour**.

You need to pay 2000 yuan **as a deposit** in advance.

We do have **free WiFi** in all our rooms, and here is our network name and WiFi password.

Practice:

Now please discuss with your classmates and talk about how to rent equipment to the guest in a business center.

Interpretation Service

Listen to the dialogue and answer the following questions:

a. What language interpreter does the guest need?
b. What are the special requirements for the interpreter?
c. When does the guest need the interpreter?
d. What's the price for the service?
e. How does the guest pay for the service?

Useful Expressions

Do you have any **special requirements**?

When will you need the interpreter?

I need to **contact** the translation company first, **for** there are no available Germany interpreters in our hotel.

The price for the service is 500 yuan **per** hour.

Would you like to **charge** it **to** your room directly?

I will inform you **as soon as** we find one for you.

Practice:

Suppose you are a clerk working in the business center in your hotel. Please read the following introduction for the translation service at your hotel and answer the questions.

The Business Center of our hotel is devoted to providing proficient translation services for our guests. The language translation service includes English, Spanish, Italian, French, Russian, Japanese, and Arabic.

For English translation service, reservations should be at least 24 hours in advance; and for other languages, it should be at least 72 hours in advance. For temporary translation, the charge is subject to the actual price of that day.

Item	Price	Contact	Service Hours
English	Inside the hotel ￥1000 / Day Inside and Outside the hotel ￥1200 / Day	Telephone: 86-519-8887**** Email: syhotel@hotmail.com	8 hours / Day
Other Languages	￥1200 ~ 1500 / Day	Telephone: 86-519-8887**** Email: syhotel@hotmail.com	

Note:
The price excludes the lunch. Please offer working lunch to the translator.

Questions

a. How many kinds of language translation does the business center provide to their guests? And what are they?
b. For French translation service, how many hours should the guest make the reservation in advance?
c. If the guest wants to have the English-Chinese interpretation service for a meeting inside the hotel for 2 days, how much will he pay for it?
d. Does the price include the lunch for the translator?
e. How does the guest contact the hotel for the translation service?

Vocabulary

broadband	[ˈbrɔːdbænd]	n.	宽带
convenient	[kənˈviːniənt]	adj.	方便的
depart	[dɪˈpɑːt]	v.	离开，出发
instruction	[ɪnˈstrʌkʃn]	n.	说明
interpreter	[ɪnˈtɜːprɪtə(r)]	n.	翻译员，口译员
interpretation	[ɪnˌtɜːprɪˈteɪʃn]	n.	翻译，解释
laptop	[ˈlæptɒp]	n.	便携式电脑，笔记本电脑
nearby	[ˌnɪəˈbaɪ]	adj.	在附近的；
		adv.	附近地
network	[ˈnetwɜːk]	n.	网络
password	[ˈpɑːswɜːd]	n.	口令，密码
rent	[rent]	n.	租金；
		v.	出租，租借
rental	[ˈrentl]	n.	租费，租金额
selection	[sɪˈlekʃn]	n.	选择，可供选择的事物
size	[saɪz]	n.	尺寸，大小
suitable	[ˈsuːtəbl]	adj.	合适的，适宜的
tablet	[ˈtæblət]	n.	平板电脑

business class	商务舱
China Eastern Airlines	中国东方航空公司
economy class	经济舱
first class	头等舱
in advance	事先，提前
pick up	开车接（某人）
rental form	租赁表格
Shanghai Pudong International Airport	上海浦东国际机场

Sanya Phoenix International Airport	三亚凤凰国际机场
WiFi (=Wireless Fidelity)	无线局域网

Exercises

I. Please translate the following sentences:

1. 5月13日有四趟航班，您什么时间合适呢？是上午还是下午？
2. 您是过来取票还是我们把票送到您的房间呢？
3. 这是租借表格以及注意事项。请您阅读一下细节并填写这份表格。
4. 我们客房里都提供免费的WiFi，这是我们的网络用户名以及WiFi密码。
5. 我们中心很多平板电脑可供选择，如苹果iPad、三星、联想、戴尔以及东芝。
6. The charge is 30 yuan an hour. You need to pay 3000 yuan as a deposit in advance.
7. I need to contact the translation company first, for there isn't any suitable Italian interpreter for you in our hotel.
8. The price for the service is 900 yuan per day. Would you like to charge it to your room directly?
9. I will inform you as soon as we find an interpreter for you.
10. How do you want your air ticket, first class, business class or economy class?

II. Role-play: Perform in pairs according to the following cards.

Guest:
Name: Peter Burts
Room Number: 603
Activity: want to book two train tickets to Xi'an
Special Requirements: afternoon, soft berth, the faster the better
Date: Thursday, September 12

Clerk:
Time: in the morning
Activity: Greet the guest, ask guest's name, room number, where to go, when to go, how many tickets, any special requirement
References: there are four times can be chosen, only two soft berth tickets left at 4:50 p.m. and need to conform early.

III. Topics for discussion

1. What information should the clerk have to make clear when the guest wants to book a train / an air ticket?
2. Can you name some kinds of certain train / air tickets?

3. What should a clerk pay attention to when the guest wants to rent equipment?
4. Is the interpretation service very necessary in the hotel? Why?
5. What transportation do you prefer when you are traveling?

An Advertisement of a Business Center

Our very complete Business Center has been organized to satisfy the needs of our business guests.

The latest in technological equipment for business meetings is added to the elegance and excellence of the service that can only be provided by the Alvear Palace Hotel.

The Business Center has the permanent assistance of professionals, and is equipped with:

6 offices with 22 flat screen computers.
Broadband Internet access and WiFi.
100MB broadband availability.
Black and white and color photocopiers.
Laser printers.
Scanner.
Flipchart.
Rental of additional technical equipment.

For those of our guests who prefer to use their own laptop we offer a special desk and WiFi.

Meeting rooms

Our hotel has meeting rooms and a board room for every type of business situation such as breakfasts, presentations, and videoconferences, amongst others.

The tables in each room have a central unit for easy broadband internet and telephone connections. The unit in the main table can be separated and rearranged to fit the requirements of the event.

These rooms are automated through an intelligent cutting-edge control system,

Acent 3, with a touch screen panel that commands the air conditioning, lighting, different preset scene projections, total or partial darkening, as well as background music.

Whenever necessary there is additional technical equipment available for rental, such as printers, computers, projectors, screens and videoconference equipment. Upon request, we offer up to 100 Mb capacity broadband at preferential rates.

Board Room

The Board Room of the Alvear Palace Hotel has a private cloakroom and restroom.

It has 6 outlets for telephone and Internet.

Technological equipment

Hitachi LCD 2500 ansi / lumen projector.

Automatic multizone DVD player.

Integrated Hi Fidelity Audio System.

Direct TV connection.

Assistance at the Business Center

A team of trained professionals offers guests assistance with the following:

Computer handling.

Internet browsing.

Fax.

Photocopying.

Black and white or color printings.

International courier service (Fedex).

Secretarial, translation and interpretation services.

CD and DVD handling techniques.

Photography downloading and copying onto CD.

Scene Four — Concierge Service

Concierge Service is very important to a hotel, for it helps in creating the most memorable experiences for guests. A hotel concierge is there to ensure that guests have everything they need during their stay. Typically, the concierge sits at a desk in the lobby, and guests can either stop by or call with their requests. In hotels, a concierge usually assists guests by performing various tasks such as making restaurant reservations, booking hotels, showing reservations, arranging for spa services, recommending night life, booking transportation, coordinating porter service, procuring of tickets to special events, recommending special gift ideas, and assisting with various travel arrangements and tours of local attractions. A concierge also assists with sending and receiving parcels and answers general questions.

English For Hotel Staff
Developing Skills
酒店实用英语（灵活应用篇）

In this unit, you will learn:

Pick-up Service

Luggage Deposit

Mail Delivery

Activities

Pick-up Service

Now you will listen to a dialogue. Decide whether the statements are True or False.

a. The guest named Lord Eric comes from Australia.

b. The guest arrives at Chengdu airport and has a very nice trip.

c. The clerk helps the guest with his three pieces of luggage.

d. This is the first time for the guest to come to Chengdu.

e. The guest can take No.902 bus to Qingcheng Mountain and No. 101 bus to Giant Panda Breeding Research Base.

f. The guest likes the hotel very much and his room number is 1635.

Useful Expressions

I hope you **had** a good trip.

Let me **help** you **with** your luggage here.

The car is waiting **outside** the airport.

We'll go to Garden Hotel **at once**.

Is this your **first trip to** Chengdu?

You can **enjoy** a day away from the city and **experience** the natural beauty of Qingcheng Mountain.

You can **take No.902 bus** to Giant Panda Breeding Research Base, or you can **take a taxi** if you want.

Dear Mr Lord, we **are arriving at** Garden Hotel.

Practice:

Please read the following information and try to answer the questions.

Blue Ocean hotel is located in Beach area, 17 kilometers from the city centre and 29 kilometers from International Airport. If you'd like to book a car to take you straight from the airport to the hotel, we can arrange a wide range of vehicles – from limousines to luggage vans. Whatever you choose, you'll find our rates very competitive. Transport to and from International Airport is complimentary for guests staying in Suites, Villas and to our Gold card holders. It is also available for all guests at an additional charge. Please allow us to help in any way we can by email or telephone number.

Option	Type of vehicles	Price per trip (RMB)
01	4-seater car	¥108
02	7-seater car	¥120
03	16-seater van	¥180
04	25-seater coach	¥360

Note:
1. Our personnel will hold a printed placard saying "Blue Ocean Hotel welcome + your name" at the airport terminal upon your arrival. DO NOT pick any other sign board that only has your name on.
2. The driver MUST show you a code that match your booking code (that we provide you with when confirming your booking). If the code doesn't match, do not leave with him.

Questions:

a. What's the location of Blue Ocean Hotel?

b. The transport is complimentary for whom?

c. If a group of guests want to be picked up by a 7-seater car at International Airport, how much will they pay for the trip?

d. How does the guest recognize the hotel personnel at the airport?

e. What kind of code should the driver show to the guest?

Luggage Deposit

Listen to the dialogue and try to fill in the following luggage deposit list.

Guest's Name:

Room Number:

Luggage Amount:

Pick-up Time:

Useful Expressions

We can **look after** your luggage **for** you.

When will you **come back for it**?

We will **arrange** the bellman to Room 808 to pick up your luggage **at once**.

Please don't forget to put your **name tag** on it.

For our guests, it's **free** for 24 hours.

We will take good care of your luggage **until** 8:00 p.m. today.

You can claim your luggage **with your ID** at our Concierge Desk in the lobby.

Practice:

Now please discuss with your classmates and try to explain the following signs in the hotel.

 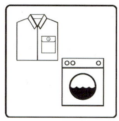  

Mail Delivery

Please complete the conversation by filling in the missing words and expressions.

(C=Clerk, G=Guest)

C: Good afternoon, sir. Is there anything I can do for you?

G: Good afternoon. I'd like to _____ to another city.

C: Certainly, sir. May I know what it is?

G: It's a brochure of our company.

C: I see. We offer two ways of delivery, _____ and _____ which usually takes 3~5 days.

G: _____ is better, because it's very urgent.

C: Ok. Please wait for a minute. Well, the charge is _____ for your express mail with one-day delivery.

G: That's OK.

C: Would you please fill in this application form with _____ and _____?

G: No problem.

C: Would you please show me your room card?

G: Here you are.

C: Thank you sir. Here is your bill. Would you like to _____ or would you like to _____?

G: Please go with my room charge.

C: Certainly, sir. I will call the Express Mail Service Company to get your mail immediately.

G: Thank you so much!

C: My pleasure. Have a nice day!

Useful Expressions

We offer **two ways of delivery**, one-day express delivery and normal delivery which usually takes 3~5 days.

Would you please fill in this **application form** with your telephone number?

Would you like to pay in cash or would you like to **charge it directly to** your room?

I will call the Express Mail Service Company to get your mail **immediately**.

Practice:

Now please discuss with your classmates and talk about how to help the guests to delivery the mail.

Vocabulary

application	[ˌæplɪˈkeɪʃn]	n.	申请
beach	[biːtʃ]	n.	海滩，海滨
claim	[kleɪm]	n.	索赔；
		v.	索要，认领，索赔
concierge	[ˈkɒnsieəʒ]	n.	礼宾部
delivery	[dɪˈlɪvəri]	n.	传送，交付
giant	[ˈdʒaɪənt]	adj.	大的，巨大的
ID	[ˌaɪ ˈdiː]	n.	身份证（identification的缩写）
immediately	[ɪˈmiːdiətli]	adv.	立即，马上
limousine	[ˈlɪməziːn]	n.	豪华轿车，接送旅客的交通车
locate	[ləʊˈkeɪt]	v.	位于

mail	[meɪl]	n.	邮件
modern	[ˈmɒdn]	adj.	现代的，近代的
mountain	[ˈmaʊntən]	n.	山，山脉
panda	[ˈpændə]	n.	熊猫
personnel	[ˌpɜːsəˈnel]	n.	人员，员工
placard	[ˈplækɑːd]	n.	标语牌，姓名牌
urgent	[ˈɜːdʒənt]	adj.	急迫的，催促的
van	[væn]	n.	厢式货车
villa	[ˈvɪlə]	n.	别墅
airport terminal			机场航站楼
at once			立刻
express mail			快件
Giant Panda Breeding Research Base			大熊猫繁育研究基地
Gold Card holder			金卡会员
pick up			接机
Qingcheng Mountain			青城山

Exercises

I. Please translate the following sentences.

1. 车正在机场外面等候，我们马上就去酒店。
2. 您可以到城市附近转一转，去黄山（Yellow Mountain）体会一下大自然的美丽。
3. 您可以乘坐302路公交车去市中心，或者您愿意的话也可以打车过去。
4. 您可以到酒店大厅里的礼宾服务台用身份证明件领取您的行李。
5. 我立刻给快件服务公司打电话来取您的邮件。
6. I hope you had a good trip. Let me help you with your luggage here.
7. Is this your first trip to Qingdao?
8. We can look after your luggage for you. When would you come back for it?
9. We will arrange the bellman to Room 2126 to pick up your luggage at once. Please don't forget to put your name tag on it.
10. Would you please fill in this application form with your telephone number?

II. Role-play: Please fill in the following luggage deposit list first and then perform in pairs according to your list.

Part 1　The Front Desk　前厅服务英语 | 29

行李寄存单

NO. _____

姓名
Name _____

联系电话
Telephone _____

行李数目
Luggage Quantity _____

日期
Date _____

时间
Time _____

房号
Room No. _____

客人签署
Guest's Signature _____

行李员签署
Bellboy's Signature _____

III. Topics for discussion

You may want to check with your hotel beforehand and see if they can pick you up at the airport. Many hotels offer a 24-hour airport transfer service and use professional and courteous drivers. A hotel pickup is obviously a very convenient service. You don't have to worry about the hotel's location. You get your price confirmed in advance, and you will probably be able to have the airport transfer charge added to your hotel bill. Please discuss with your partner about the following pictures and try to explain the following types of vehicles.

a. _____　b. _____　c. _____

d. _____　e. _____　f. _____

g. _____   h. _____   i. _____

Tips

The Concierge Service in a Hotel

In hotels, the knowledgeable and amiable Concierges are delighted to help their guests in any way possible throughout their stay.

Services include:
- Airline schedules and reservations.
- Area maps.
- Audio, visual and business equipment.
- Automobile rental.
- Babysitting services.
- Cellular phone needs.
- Dog-walking services.
- Facsimile, (FAX)
- Limousine service, transportation.
- Mail, messages, shipping.
- Massages and personal fitness training.
- Medical and dental assistance.
- Notary public.
- Pharmacy assistance.
- Photocopies.
- Religious services.
- Restaurant reservations.
- Secretarial services.
- Shopping information.
- Taxis.
- Theater service.
- Travel arrangements.

Scene Five — The Cashier

A hotel cashier refers to a staff working at the Front Desk, who collects money from guests for their lodging accommodations and any other fees they may incur during their stay, including parking, valet, room service and telephone or computer use fees. He/she is also commonly required to maintain records and files regarding financial transactions that take place at the front desk. Good mathematical skills are required for this job. Although most modern cash registers or point-of-sale（POS机，刷卡机）terminals automatically calculate fees and taxes based on the software, a hotel cashier is expected to be able to accurately calculate room rates or discounts. He/she may also perform a variety of banking services for guests, and may handle cash, traveller's cheque, credit cards, foreign currency exchange, as well as direct billing requests properly. Customer service skills are needed for this job, as well as the ability to work well with other hotel staff personnel.

In this unit, you will learn:

Credit Card Payment

Cash Payment

Foreign Currency Exchange

Activities

Credit Card Payment

Now you will listen to a dialogue between a cashier and a guest. Decide whether the statements are True or False.

a. The guest is Peter Singh from room 1240.
b. The guest didn't use the mini-bar this morning.

c. The bill totals RMB 1290, including a 10% service charge.
d. The guest doesn't want to pay in cash because he doesn't have enough cash.
e. The hotel can accept all kinds of credit cards.
f. The guest paid the bill by American Express card.

Useful Expressions

Have you used the mini-bar or other services this morning?
Please wait for a moment, I'll **print the bill** for you.
Yes, we **do accept** some major credit cards, such as American Express, Visa or MasterCard.
We hope you will be staying with us **again**.

Practice:

Please look at the following logos of the popular ways of payment, and try to explain them one by one.

a. _____   b. _____   c. _____

d. _____   e. _____   f. _____

Cash Payment

Listen to the dialogue and answer the following questions:

a. What's the name and the room number of the guest?
b. How do you ask the guest to give you back the room card?
c. What is the cost of the total bill?
d. How does the guest settle her account?
e. How much is the deposit of the guest and how much is the change?

Useful Expressions

May I have your **key card**, please?

I'll **draw up** your bill for you.

How will you by **settling your account**?

May I have **the receipt from** your deposit?

You paid **a deposit of** RMB 2000.

Here is your invoice and your **change**, 130 yuan.

Practice:

What are the same steps and different steps on serving guests between credit card payment and cash payment?

Foreign Currency Exchange

Please complete the conversation by filling in the missing words and expressions.

(C=Cashier, G=Guest)

C: Good morning, sir. May I help you?

G: Yes. Can I change some _____ here?

C: Certainly, sir. What kind of foreign currency have you got, sir?

G: _____. What's the exchange rate today?

C: According to today's exchange rate, one dollar is equivalent to _____. How much would you like to change, sir?

G: _____. Here is the money.

C: May I see your passport, please?

G: Here you are.

C: Now here is the _____ for you. Please fill in this form with your _____, your _____, the _____ and your _____.

G: Sure.

C: And please sign your name here.

G: Is that all right?

C: Yes, that's good. Here is _____ for you. Please have a check and keep the exchange memo.

G: By the way, what should I do with the remaining Renminbi?

C: You can go to several specialized foreign exchange banks to change it back, like Bank of China, China Construction Bank, Industrial and Commercial Bank of China, or you can go to the airport _____, too.

G: I see. Thank you for your information.

C: That's my pleasure.

Useful Expressions

What kind of **foreign currency** have you got, sir?

According to today's **exchange rate**, one dollar **is equivalent to** 6.36 yuan.

How much would you like to **change**, sir?

Here is the **exchange rate memo** for you.

Please **have a check** and keep the exchange memo.

You can go to the **foreign exchange bank** to change it back, or you can go to the **airport exchange office**, too.

Practice:

Suppose you are a cashier working in Holly Hotel in Shanghai. This afternoon a guest comes to your desk and wants to exchange 200 US dollars into Chinese Renminbi. Please fill in the exchange memo first and try to make up a dialogue according to the memo.

```
                The Grand Stanford Hotel
                 Fifth Avenue, New York

Purchased from: _____Candice Lee_____
Room: _2879_ Passport No: _********_

    Currency Amount      Exchange Rate       US $ Equivalent
                           RMB 3000                6.34
    $ 473.19

                    Guest's Signature: Candice Lee
                    Authority Signature & Stamp:    *
```

Vocabulary

according	[əˈkɔːdɪŋ]	v.	使符合；
		adv.	依照
dollar	[ˈdɒlə(r)]	n.	美元
equivalent	[ɪˈkwɪvələnt]	adj.	相等的，等价的
exchange	[ɪksˈtʃeɪndʒ]	v.	交换，兑换
foreign	[ˈfɒrən]	adj.	外国的，外来的
major	[ˈmeɪdʒə(r)]	adj.	主要的，重要的
memo	[ˈmeməʊ]	n.	备忘录
remain	[rɪˈmeɪn]	n.	剩余的物品，没用掉的东西；
		v.	保持，保留
settle	[ˈsetl]	v.	解决，安排，处理

specialize	['speʃəlaɪz]	v.	专门

airport exchange office	机场外币兑换处
Bank of China	中国银行
China Construction Bank	中国建设银行
Industrial and Commercial Bank of China	中国工商银行
be equivalent to ...	等同于，相当于……
draw up	整理
exchange memo	兑换水单
exchange rate	兑换率
foreign currency	外币

Exercise

I. Please translate the following sentences:
1. 是的，我们确实接受常见的信用卡，如美国运通卡，维萨卡或者万事达卡。
2. 可以把您的房卡给我吗？我来结下您的账单。
3. 您付了1500元押金，这是您的发票和68元找零。
4. 根据今天的兑换率，1美金折合人民币6.36元。
5. 您可以去中国银行兑换，或者您可以去机场的外币兑换处。
6. Please wait for a moment, I'll print the bill for you.
7. How will you settle your account?
8. What kind of foreign currency have you got, sir?
9. How much would you like to change, sir?
10. Here is the exchange memo for you. Please have a check.

II. Role-play: Read the Foreign Exchange memo and try to explain the details. Then make up a dialogue according to the information given below.

The Grand Stanford Hotel
Fifth Avenue, New York

Purchased from: ___Candice Lee___
Room: __2879__   Passport No: __*********__

Currency Amount	Exchange Rate	US$ Equivalent
RMB 3000	6.34	$ 473.19

Guest's Signature: ___Candice Lee___
Authority Signature & Stamp: ___*___

III. Now you are checking a guest out. Please read the following responses from the guest and try your best to check the guest out. Then compare your conversation with your partners.

Guest: Good morning. I'd like to check out, please.
You: (*Please respond to the request and ask for name and room number.*)
Guest: Mary Williams. Room 456.
You: (*Present the bill to her, tell her the total number is 1089 yuan, and ask her to check the bill.*)
Guest: That looks all correct.
You: (*Ask guest the way to pay the bill.*)
Guest: With my Visa card.
You: (*Ask guest for credit card.*)
Guest: Here you are.
You: (*Ask her for signature.*)
Guest: Sure. Here it is.
You: (*Give the card and the invoice back to her and extend the wishes.*)
Guest: Thank you. I am sure I will be back.

What should a cashier know about these modes of payment?

Credit Card

It is amongst the most favored modes of account settlement. While processing a payment through credit card the front office cashier follows the following procedures:

1. Check the card holder's name, expiry date and the credit limit of the card.
2. Swipe the card for verification and authorization from the issuer of the card.
3. Ask the guest to sign on the transaction slip.
4. Return the credit card and a copy of the transaction slip to the guest.

Traveler's Cheque

It is issued by a financial institution and functions as cash but is protected against loss or theft. While accepting a traveler's cheque from a guest the front desk cashier should proceed as follows:

1. Ensure that the second signature is put in front of him.

2. Check the guest's passport to establish identity and write the passport number behind the traveler's cheque.

3. Calculate the correct exchange value if the traveler's cheque is in foreign currency.

4. Return the balance to the guest in local currency.

Cash

It is the best method of payment especially for unknown guests or those with little luggage.

Debit Card

It is a plastic card that allows customers to access their funds immediately, electronically. It is a safe mode of account settlement as the amount is instantly transferred to the hotel's account.

Personal Cheques

These may be accepted by the hotel from known guests who have already established their credentials with the hotel. Proper identification like driving license, passport, etc is required. This type of payment has to be authorized by the lobby manger.

Corporate Billing

Executives, who travel at the expense of the company or for company work, charge their expenses directly to the company. They make a deal with the hotel, whereby they determine the rates for different types of rooms and meal plans to be offered to their executives. The terms and conditions of the payment are also predetermined. The executives carry a letter from their company, which is called a Bill to Company (BTC) letter as a proof of identity.

Alipay

It is the independent third-party payment platform, founded by Alibaba group. Pay treasure to provide China's e-commerce "simple, safe, fast," online payment solutions.

Alipay method:

1. open the bank on the net

2. opened alipay

3. Use the net bank card to recharge to alipay

4. Then confirm the delivery of buyer, taobao will play money to the seller.

WeChat Pay

WeChat Pay empowers merchants to connect with consumers before, during, and after sales through innovative marketing platforms in the WeChat ecosystem.

1. User opens WeChat and displays their Quick Pay code.

2. Merchant scans Quick Pay code.

3. Payment is completed and confirmation sent to the merchant and user.

笔记 | Notes

Part 2

Housekeeping Department
客房服务英语

Brainstorm

Please look at the picture of the chamber service in this hotel, and describe what job functions are there in Housekeeping Department. As a class, list the words that describe the possible staff, services, amenities or facilities this hotel might have. Then discuss them with your groups. See which group has the largest vocabulary.

people, places, things, services ...

Scene One

Chamber Service

Chamber service is a job performed by room attendants or housekeepers, who clean up after guests leave and prepare the rooms for new guests. Room attendants must ensure privacy and confidentiality for guests, in addition to addressing questions and concerns and reporting maintenance issues or other problems. A room attendant's job consists of cleaning hotel rooms from top to bottom, both during a guest's stay and in preparation for the next guest. They clean all surfaces and replace bed linen, then move on to the bathroom, where they replace the towels and clean showers, bathtubs and toilets. After finishing the bathroom, the attendant typically vacuums before leaving the room. Though chamber service is usually associated with cleaning, the attendants or housekeepers also interact with guests, handling complaints and answering questions.

In this unit, you will learn:

Cleaning the Room

Turn-down Service

Adding Beds

Activities

Cleaning the Room

Listen to the dialogue and answer the following questions:

a. What does the guest need for his room?
b. Where can the guest find the umbrella in his room?
c. What does the guest require to take his medicine?
d. Does the guest need extra covers?
e. How will the housekeeping clean the room?

Useful Expressions

May I clean your room now?
It's raining outside now, **there is an umbrella in your closet**.
Do you need **fresh sheets**?
The sheets **will be OK** for another night.
I need some hot water to **wash down my medicine**.
It's getting cold, do you need **extra covers**?
I will **vacuum your room** and **make your bed** later.

Practice:

There are some tips for efficiently cleaning a bathroom. Read some of the tips below and put the procedures in the correct order.

1. Scrub the bowl with a toilet brush and flush.
2. Remove all the items that don't belong to the bathroom.
3. Clean the sink and counter area.
4. Pour some bleach or disinfectant into the toilet bowl.
5. Apply any scrub powder to especially dirty areas.
6. Sweep and mop the floor.
7. Clean the shower.

Turn-down Service

Listen to the dialogue and mark the following sentences with True or False.

1. It is time for the room attendant to do the room service, but the guest refuses at first.
2. The guest requests the room attendant to come back in three hours, so the room attendant leaves.
3. The guest wants to have the bathroom cleaned because she just had a shower and the

bathroom is in a mess.

4. The room attendant is asked to get some boiled water because the guest is thirsty.
5. The guest's friends will stay overnight in the hotel.
6. The room attendant drew the curtains to make a cozy setting for the guests.
7. When the guest's friends arrive, the bellman will guide them to the room.

Useful Expressions

May I **do the turn-down service** for you now?
Could you **come back in three hours**?
I'll let the overnight staff know. They will come then.
Would you **tidy up a bit** in the bathroom?
We'd **treat our friends to typical Chinese tea**.
I'll bring in some fresh towels **together with** boiled water.
If your friends like to **stay overnight**, please let me know to book rooms for them !
Would you like me to draw the curtains for you, sir and madam?
May I turn on the lights for you?
When your friends arrive, the bellman will **guide them to your room**.
Have a very pleasant evening.

Practice:

Discuss what the job of turn-down service is.

Adding Beds

Listen to a conversation. Please fill in the missing words and expressions as you listen to the dialogue.
Scene: A guest is calling room center for an extra bed.

(R=Receptionist, G=Guest)

R: Good afternoon. Room center. Anna speaking. How can I help you?
G: Good afternoon, this is Mrs. Evans _____. My daughter will be staying with me tonight, so I need _____ in my room.
R: OK. We can bring up a fold-out bed for you, madam.
G: Thank you. My daughter is bringing her baby, so I will also _____.
R: That's no problem. May I know how old the baby is _____?
G: The baby is one year old .
R: We have the right size cot for the baby .
G: Can you put _____ in my wardrobe.
R: Yes, of course.
G: Will you bring _____ for the extra bed?
R: Yes, of course.
G: How much should I pay for those?

R: The extra bed is RMB500 yuan per night while others are free. The charge will be _____. The bellman will send the bill for you to sign in 10 minutes. Will that be all right?

G: All right.

R: Do you need _____?

G: Yes, please.

R: Is there anything else I can help with?

G: Could you please make sure _____ so the baby can sleep well?

R: Certainly, no one will disturb you, madam. Anything else, madam?

G: Nothing else. Thank you very much.

R: You're welcome. We are always at your service.

Useful Expressions

I **need an extra bed** in my room.

We can bring up **a fold-out bed** for you, madam.

May I know how old the baby is so as to provide the exact cot?

Will you bring **sheets and bedding for the extra bed**?

The extra bed is **RMB 500 yuan per night** while others are free.

The charge will **be billed to your room account**.

The bellman will send **the bill for you to sign** in 10 minutes.

Certainly, no one will disturb you, madam.

Practice:

Discuss the procedures of adding a bed.

Vocabulary

bedding	['bedɪŋ]	n.	寝具，铺盖
blanket	['blæŋkɪt]	n.	毯子
conditioner	[kən'dɪʃənə]	n.	护发素
cover	['kʌvə]	n.	被子，封面
cozy	['kəʊzɪ]	adj.	舒适的，惬意的
cot	[kɒt]	n.	婴儿床
curtain	['kɜ:tn]	n.	窗帘
messy	['mesi]	adj.	混乱的，肮脏的
shampoo	[ʃæm'pu:]	n.	洗发水
sheet	[ʃi:t]	n.	被单
towel	['taʊəl]	n.	毛巾

| vacuum | ['vækjuəm] | v. | 吸尘 |
| wardrobe | ['wɔ:drəub] | n. | 衣柜 |

a flask of			一瓶
baby shampoo			婴儿洗发露
bill to room account			挂房账
fold-out bed			折叠床
overnight staff			夜班服务员
toilet roll			卷纸
turndown service			做晚床
treat... to...			用……款待……

Exercises

I. Please translate the following sentences:
1. 我们可以为您拿张折叠床上来。
2. 早上好！客房打扫，可以进来吗？
3. 每张加床每晚收费300元人民币。
4. 我马上为您的房间吸尘，然后铺床。
5. 很抱歉，打扰了！现在可以为您打扫房间吗？
6. I'll get another hair-dryer for you.
7. May I move the things on your desk so that I can dust it?
8. The fact is that turn-down service normally doesn't take a lot of time. We always indicate rooms to be made up in advance on request.
9. What time would you like me to come back to clean your room?
10. Some hotels will put a bar of chocolate on the pillow to wish guest "sweet dreams".

II. Choose the names of items that match the pictures, and write them down under the pictures.

| towel | bathrobe | toilet roll | toiletries | bedside lamp | pillow & quilt |
| drink packets | cups | safe | rubbish bin | hair-dyer | slippers |

a._____ b._____ c._____ d._____

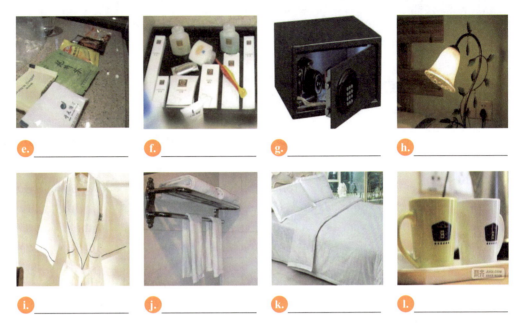

e. _____ f. _____ g. _____ h. _____

i. _____ j. _____ k. _____ l. _____

III. Read the following passage and decide whether the statements are true or false. Write T for true and F for false.

Efficiently managed Housekeeping Departments ensure the cleanliness, maintenance, and aesthetic appeal of hotels. The Housekeeping Department not only prepares clean guest rooms on a timely basis for arriving guests, it also cleans and maintains everything in the hotel so that the property is as fresh and attractive as the day it opened for business.

Housekeeping Department usually has more employees than any other hotel department. Besides the management staff, there are employees assigned to clean guest rooms, public spaces, back-of-the-house areas, meeting rooms, and banquet rooms. Some hotels have employees working in night cleaning and linen and laundry rooms, while in the other hotels, these areas are covered by contractors.

The tasks performed by a Housekeeping Department are critical to the smooth daily operation of any hotel. The primary communications of Housekeeping Department are with Front Office Department and Maintenance Department. At most properties, the reception agent is not allowed to assign guest rooms until the rooms have been cleaned, inspected and released by the Housekeeping Department. Maintenance Department has similar goals and methods as Housekeeping Department. Hence, a close working relationship is very important.

1. _____ Housekeeping Department is only responsible for cleaning guest rooms.
2. _____ Housekeeping Department usually has more employees than any other hotel department.
3. _____ The tasks performed by a Housekeeping Department are very important to operate the hotel smoothly.
4. _____ Housekeeping works closer to Front Office than to Maintenance Department.

5. _____ The reception agent can assign guest rooms when the rooms are being cleaned.

Hotel Bed Making Procedures

Every hotel has its own way of folding linens and making the beds. Procedures come down from management and are carried out by housekeeping so that every room has the same distinct feel. Hotel beds are made to the exact specifications every time and, once housekeepers understand the process, it becomes a simple and effective way to make each room uniform.

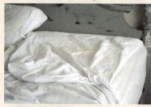

Start Fresh
Strip the bed of the sheets, pillowcases, blankets and comforter. If the bed is near the wall, pull it out so you can easily reach behind it. Place the soiled linens in a bag to bring back to laundry.

Layer it Up
Place the clean linens on a bench or chair and refer to the bed-making card or outline until you're confident you can make the bed to the hotel's exact specifications. Some hotels add an additional layer of mattress protector, a boxed feather bed or a felt sheet protector. Make sure these items are in place first before attempting to place the sheets on the bed.

Bottom Sheet
Spread a fitted sheet onto the bed or lay a flat sheet on top of the mattress. Pull the fitted sheet onto a corner and secure near the bottom of the mattress. Repeat on the other three corners. Otherwise, spread the flat sheet out and make "hospital corners" or follow the specific folding method the hotel requires.

Top Sheet
Place a face-down top sheet over the bottom sheet and tuck all the edges in just as you did the bottom sheet. Allow about one foot of extra fabric at the head of the bed. Add a light blanket if necessary and tuck in everywhere as directed. Fold the top sheet back and over the blanket. Tuck everything in underneath the mattress.

Pillows and Blankets
When the bed is made, slip clean pillowcases over the pillows. Arrange the pillows on top of the comforter to meet hotel expectations. Pay particular attention to smoothing out wrinkles and making sure

> each pillow looks distinctively placed. Add an additional folded blanket at the end of the bed, provided the hotel requests this. If not, placing an extra blanket in the closet is a nice touch in case guests get cold.

Scene Two — Laundry Service

The Housekeeping Department is the backbone of a hotel. The main duty of the staff is to see to the cleanliness and good order of all rooms and public areas in the hotel. The laundry service is also part of their job. They should not only keep the bed linen, table linen and work clothing clean, but also wash, press, and repair clothes for guests according to their laundry lists. They ensure clean, fresh clothing is available at all times to make sure the guests are satisfied and the hotel keeps running smoothly.

In this unit, you will learn:

Express Service

Special Requirements

Laundry Damage

Activities

Express Service

Listen to the dialogue about Express Service and finish the information in the form below.

Guest's Name:
Room Number:
Items to Be Cleaned:
Method of Cleaning:
Charge :
Payment:
Time The Laundry Will Be Returned:

Useful Expressions

I need to **get my suit cleaned** right away.

Do you have a **dry cleaning service**?

But we usually **pick up laundry** before 9:00 a.m. Now it's 10:00. I'm afraid your laundry can't be returned today.

How much do you charge for the express service?

There is an **extra charge of** 50% for the express service.

We can **add it to your room account**.

When can it **be returned**?

I will send the bellman to **pick up the car key from your room** now.

Practice:

List some expressions used to introduce the laundry service and express service.

Special Requirements

Listen to the dialogue about some special requirements for laundry service and answer the following questions:

a. What's the problem with the guest's trousers?

b. Can the trousers be repaired before tomorrow morning?

c. What kind of stain is it on the trousers?

d. What's the guest's concern about washing the dress?

e. What suggestion is given to the guest about writing the laundry list?

Useful Expressions

Do you **do repairs to clothes**?

I have some trousers that **need repairing**.

We can usually repair clothes within two days, but **it depends on how serious the damage is**.

I'll **send someone up** in a few minutes.

If they have a look at them, **they'll tell you how long it will take**.

What kind of stain is it, sir?

We'll **do our best to remove the stain**.

My wife needs her dress washed, but I'm afraid **the color will run in the wash**.

But you will need to **write down special instructions** on your laundry list.

Practice:

Make up a dialogue about laundry service, based on the information you need from the form below.

Items	Requirements
Sweater	Hand-wash
Suit	Machine-wash
Overcoat	Laundry
Blouse	Dry-clean
Tie	Starch
Shirt	Bleach
Dress	Stain-remove
Jacket	Iron/Press
Trousers	Repair

Laundry Damage

Listen to a conversation and complete it by filling in the missing words and expressions as you listen to the dialogue.

Scene: A laundryman comes to the guest's room to return the dress and apologizes for the laundry damage. The guest asks for compensation.

(L= laundryman, G=Guest)

L: Laundry service. May I come in?

G: Come in, please.

L: Thank you. I've brought up the clothes _____. But I'm awfully sorry that there is a little _____. Your silk dress was a little bit burnt due to _____. We do apologize for this.

G: Oh, my God! Let me have a look at it. I was told your Laundry Department had _____ in this work. How could this happen?

L: We're so sorry. It's our mistake.

G: This is a new dress. I just bought it and cost me quite a lot. Does your hotel have _____?

L: According to the hotel policies, we should pay for the damage, but the indemnity should not exceed _____. I hope you understand us.

G: What's the laundry charge?

L: 35 yuan. It's on the laundry list.

G: 35 yuan? That means I can only get 350 yuan _____. Are you kidding? The dress cost me 880 yuan! It's unfair.

L: I'm sorry. _____.

G: I'm not satisfied. I want to see your manager.

L: In that case, I'll get the manager to take care of the issue. Sorry to have caused you so much trouble.

Useful Expressions

But **I'm awfully sorry that** there is a little **laundry damage**.
Your silk dress was a little bit burnt due to **overheating of the iron**.
We **do apologize for** this.
We're so sorry. It's our mistake.
Does your hotel have **a policy on dealing with this kind of thing**?
According to the hotel policies, we should pay for the damage, but the **indemnity should not exceed 10 times the laundry charge.**
In that case, I'll get the manager to **take care of the issue**.
Sorry to have caused you so much trouble.

Practice:

Write out the correct word according to the first letter.

1. What if there is any laundry d_____?
2. The dress is a little bit burnt due to o_____ of the iron.
3. Does your hotel have a p_____ on dealing with it?
4. Under this agreement, they were to pay an i_____ for five million dollars.
5. He paid a sum of money as a c_____ for the loss in the fire.
6. The r_____ has no application to this particular case.

Vocabulary

instruction	[ɪnˈstrʌkʃn]	n.	指示，使用说明，操作指南
indemnity	[ɪnˈdemnəti]	n.	赔偿，赔偿金
iron	[ˈaɪən]	n.	熨斗
overheat	[ˌəʊvəˈhiːt]	v.	使过热
remove	[rɪˈmuːv]	v.	去除
spill	[spɪl]	v.	溢出，泼出
split	[splɪt]	v.	分裂，分开
stain	[steɪn]	n.	污渍
dry cleaning service			干洗服务
express service			快洗服务
laundry damage			洗衣损坏
laundry service			洗衣服务
soy sauce			酱油

Exercises

I. Please translate the following sentences:

1. 请派人来取我要送洗的衣物好吗?
2. 我需要把这件外套干洗。
3. 可以填写一下洗衣单吗?
4. 它可能会缩水，所以请用冷水手洗。
5. 我们会努力除去这个污点，但无法保证结果。
6. I'm afraid it's too late for today's laundry.
7. The cost of the express service is 100% more than the ordinary laundry service.
8. We also have an express laundry service, and it takes only three hours.
9. The items in your bag don't match up with the items on the laundry list.
10. We made a mistake while delivering your shirt. We're very sorry for the inconvenience.

II. Role-play: Make up a dialogue according to the situation below.

> **Situation:**
> **Guest:** You complain about the laundry service in the hotel for your clothes have been misdelivered for two times.
> **Clerk:** You are a hotel clerk in the housekeeping department. Try to deal with it right away and make sure to reach a satisfactory solution.

III. Look at the sample laundry operational flow chart below and try to describe the hotel laundry operation.

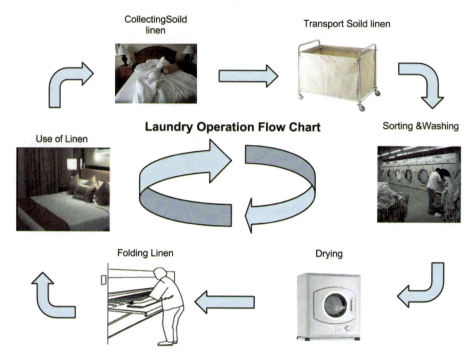

Sample Laundry operational flow chart

 Tips

Laundry Service Procedures

1. When Guest requests the laundry service, the Service Center will direct the guest to fill out the laundry list first, and designate the return time needed. Then contact the floor attendant to collect.

2. When guest requests other housekeeping services, Service Center must get the guest request information accurately and quickly, and contact the right attendant.

3. All requests must be properly logged, delivered and followed up, to ensure guest satisfaction.

4. If guests complain about laundry service:

◆ **When laundry is not returned**

Service Center Staff apologizes to the guest first, confirms guest's name and room number and whether the guest has searched the wardrobe, if not found then inform laundry to check and call guest back for an update.

◆ **When laundry is delivered to the wrong room**

If delivery of incorrect garments to the guest's room, Service Center Staff should thank the guest to inform us, and inform the laundry shift leader to collect immediately. If the guest's garments are delivered to wrong room, apologize first, confirm guest's name & room number, then inform Laundry shift leader to check, and call back to the guest.

◆ **If some laundry is missing**

Service Center Staff should apologize to the guest first, write down guest's name and room number, and confirm missed garment and laundry date, and confirm whether the guest have searched the wardrobe, then call Guest Service Manager immediately

◆ **If the laundry is damaged**

Service Center Staff should apologize to the guest first, write down guest's name and room number, and call Guest Service Manager immediately.

5. Service Center Staff should be familiar with the use of the room facilities and the items, and make a file , update if there is any change , and share with other sections correctly the first time, especially for the operator.

Scene Three — Personal Service

An upscale full service hotel offers not only luxury amenities, full service accommodations, full service restaurant(s), but also the highest level of personalized and professional services, such as wake-up service, shoe shining service, baby-sitting service, maintenance service, fax service, ticket booking service, translation service etc. Luxury hotels go out of their way to please their guests by providing all the comforts of home throughout their trips. In most cases, they even find themselves more comfortable and pampered in the hotel. The luxury hotel has become, in a very real sense is, " A home away from home."

In this unit, you will learn:

Wake-up Service

Shoe-shining Service

Baby-sitting Service

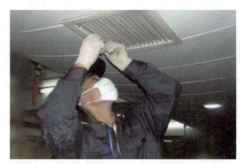
Maintenance Service

Activities

Wake-up Service

Listen to a conversation. A guest is calling for a wake-up call service. Please complete it by filling in the missing words and expressions as you listen to the dialogues.

Scene: A guest calls for a wake-up call service, and the operator answers the phone.

(O= Operator, G=Guest)

O: Good evening._____. May I help you?

G: Good evening. This is Mr. Black _____. I was wondering if your hotel had a wake up call service.

O: Yes, sir. What kind of call would you prefer, _____ by the computer wake-up system, or _____?

G: By phone, please.

O: What time would you like to be woken up?

G: 6:30 a.m. I need to _____.

O: OK. We will wake you up at 6:30 tomorrow morning, sir.

G: Don't forget, please.

O: _____. We won't forget. Have a good sleep.

G: Thank you.

…

(6:30 next morning)

O: Good morning, Mr. Black. It's 6:30. You asked me to wake you up.

G: Oh, yes, thank you. Could you please _____ to take me to the station?

O: Sure, sir. What time do you need the cab to be ready?

G: 7:45 will be good.

O: You will find the cab ready _____ on time. Would you like me to send the bellman to _____?

G: No, thanks. I can handle it. Can you please tell me how the weather is today?

O: Today is a sunny day, warm and the temperature is _____.

G: Nice. Thanks a lot.

O: My pleasure. Have a nice day!

Useful Expressions

I was wondering if your hotel had a **wake up call service**.

What kind of call would you prefer, **by phone, by the computer wake-up system, or by knocking at the door**?

What time would you like to be woken up?

It's 6:30. You asked me **to wake you up**.

Could you please **order a cab** to take me to the station?

You will find the cab ready at the front door on time.

Would you like me to **send the bellman to help you with the luggage**?

Today is a sunny day, warm and **the temperature is 25 degrees outside**.

Practice:

Miss Liu asks for a wake-up call at 6:00 tomorrow morning, because she needs to attend a meeting in another city. Make up a dialogue based on the useful sentences above.

Shoe-shining Service

Listen to the dialogue about shoe-shining service and answer the following questions:

a. How does the hotel offer the shoe-shining service?
b. Where in the room can the guest find the shoe-shining equipment?
c. How long does it take to use the shoe-shining machine?
d. Is shoe-shining service free or not?
e. What does the guest need for his mini-bar?

Useful Expressions

I need to **have my shoes polished**. Do you have a **shoe-shining service**?

There's **shoe-shining** materials in the wardrobe. We also have a **shoe-shining machine**.

If you like, I'll send someone up to **take your shoes to the shoe polishing room**.

When can I **get** my shoes **back**?

By the way, is it **complimentary** or do I **need to pay for it**?

Could you **get some more drinks in the mini-bar** of my room?

The room attendant **will be up in a minute**.

Practice:

Introduce the shoe-shining service to the guest.

Baby-sitting Service

Listen to the dialogue and mark the following sentences with T (true) or F (false).

1. _____ The parents need a baby-sitting service because they are going out tonight.
2. _____ The room attendant agrees to look after the children.
3. _____ The Kid's Club is a place where kids can play and watch movies together.
4. _____ The hotel will send a baby sitter to the guests' room.
5. _____ There's usually a confirmation form to sign before using a baby-sitting service.

Useful Expressions

But I'm afraid that's impossible. **It's against our hotel regulations** for me to do this service.

Our Housekeeping Department has **a very good baby-sitting service**.

The baby-sitters are **well-trained and reliable**.

They can go to the Kid's Club or we can **send a baby sitter to your room**.

It's a place where children can play and watch movies together.

If you ask the Housekeeping, they will **give you more details and send a confirmation form for you to sign**.

Practice:

Discuss the procedures of baby-sitting service and put the procedures in the correct order.

a. Hotel staff checks the application form, especially the guest's contact number, kid's living habits, dos and don'ts when serving.
b. Guest asks hotel for baby-sitting service in advance if necessary.
c. Baby-sitter takes care of the kids with care.
d. Guest fills in the application form of baby-sitting service.
e. Baby-sitter returns the kid to the guest and asks the guest to sign the bill.
d. Hotel arranges a baby-sitter.

Maintenance Service

Listen to the dialogue about maintenance service and answer the following questions:

a. Who is the guest? In which room is the guest in?

b. What's wrong with the air-conditioner?
c. What does the repairman do to the remote control?
d. What's wrong with the toilet?
e. Has the repairman fixed the toilet?

Useful Expressions

I have a problem with the air-conditioner in my room and the toilet doesn't flush.
Could you **send someone** to repair them?
I'm sorry to hear that. **We'll send someone up** to check immediately.
Maintenance. May I come in?
Could you tell me what the trouble is in detail?
Let me have a look at the remote control, please.
I think the batteries should be changed. **Let me replace them with new ones**.
Yes, **the toilet doesn't flush**. I'm afraid **it's clogged**.
The toilet is all right now. **You may try it**.

Practice:

Make a dialogue according to the following situation.
Guest: The desk lamp doesn't work and the water tap in the room is dripping all the time.
Staff: You change the light bulb for the desk lamp and replace some parts of the water tap. The problems are solved.

Vocabulary

battery	[ˈbætri]	n.	电池
cab	[kæb]	n.	出租车
maintenance	[ˈmeɪntənəns]	n.	维修，保养
mini-bar	[ˈmɪnibɑː(r)]	n.	迷你吧
polish	[ˈpɒlɪʃ]	v.	擦光，润色
tin	[tɪn]	n.	罐头盒
wardrobe	[ˈwɔːdrəub]	n.	衣柜，衣橱
remote	[rɪˈməut]	n.	远程操作，遥控器
air-conditioner		n.	空调
baby-sitting service			托婴服务
baby sitter			照顾婴儿者
computer wake-up system			电脑叫醒系统
mineral water			矿泉水

58 English For Hotel Staff
Developing Skills　酒店实用英语（灵活应用篇）

hotel regulations	酒店规章制度
remote control	遥控器
shoe-shining service	擦鞋服务
shoe-shiner	擦鞋器
shoe-shining machine	擦鞋机
wake-up call service	叫醒服务

Exercises

I. Please translate the following sentences:
1. 您需要明早几点叫醒？
2. 我们会马上派人来修的。
3. 我需要擦鞋，你们有擦鞋服务吗？
4. 我房间里的抽水马桶好像出了点毛病。
5. 我可以向您推荐我们部门的托儿服务吗？
6. Our room attendant will wake you up at 6:30 tomorrow morning.
7. The water tap drips all night long.
8. Some parts needs to be replaced. I will be back soon.
9. There are some experienced baby-sitters in the Baby-sitting Center.
10. The Baby-sitting service charges 20 yuan per hour, with a minimum of 4 hours.

II. Write out questions according to the answers.
1. _____
   I would like to be woken up at 5:30 tomorrow morning.
2. _____
   The toilet doesn't flush and the shower head keeps dripping.
3. _____
   I'm afraid you have to wait for twenty minutes.
4. _____
   Yes. We have a baby-sitting service from 10 a.m. to 9 p.m.
5. _____
   It's Mr. Shawn in Room 1822.
6. _____
   It's complimentary.

III. Write a composition with the title "Best Service Provided to My Guests".

How to Make a Great Hotel Service?
Many of us luxury travelers believe that service makes the difference between

a very nice hotel and A memorable hotel. But what constitutes truly great luxury hotel service?

1. An Available Hotel General Manager or Resident Manager

He or she should be out on the floor greeting guests and putting a face on hotel operations. Connected, committed, one-on-one hotel service *starts at the top* and sets the tone for the entire hotel.

2. Personality

Hospitality personality goes further than cheerfulness. A great, five-star hotel employee also thinks things through. He or she has a sense of priority, attention to detail, practicality, follow-through and efficiency.

3. Check-in, Check-out

Check-in should be personalized, quick, genuinely friendly, and thorough. A guest's first contact with the hotel is the valet, doorman, and bellman. These staffers must communicate welcome, in words, smiles, actions and body language.

4. Discretion with Names

Knowing guests' names and correct titles is a good thing, and makes the guests feel valued.

5. Observe, Don't Presume

The guest should feel in command and not dictated to. Hotel staff should never presume they know a guest's taste. They should ask questions, give options, and let the guest decide.

6. Room Service

Room service can be exquisite and personalized, or perfunctory and mediocre.

7. Housekeeping

The best housekeeping personnel are extremely observant and not assumptive. They can rearrange things slightly, but should never move the guests' possessions. And they should not take away anything unless it's in the garbage or recycling bin.

8. Complete Mastery of the Hotel and Locale

A fine hotel's staffers do not wear blinders. They should be able to tell a guest where everything is situated in the hotel: services, dining, entertainment. They should know hours, charges, policies.

笔记 | Notes

Food & Beverage Department
餐饮服务英语

Part 3

Brainstorm

Please look at the picture of the restaurant in this hotel, and describe how the restaurant looks. Work with your partner, and try to answer the following questions:

a. How many kinds of restaurant staff do you know? What are they?
b. What services does a hotel restaurant usually offer?

Then discuss them with your classmates.

staff, services ...

Scene One

Welcoming Guests

As a host or hostess, you are the first and last person guests see at a restaurant. Because of this, you must always try your best to leave a good impression to your guests. While welcoming them to the restaurant and asking how they're doing can seem redundant to you, your patrons may see you as rude if you don't ask these typical questions. When a guest arrives at your restaurant, an effective server is able to check to see if the guest does in fact have a reservation for that time and communicate with guests without being hurried. Keeping the restaurant orderly, making sure guests are happy, and keeping track of what's going on at each table are just some of the ways you can keep your guests happy.

In this unit, you will learn:

Serving Reserved Guests

Serving Non-reserved Guests

Changing the Table

Activities

Serving Reserved Guests

Listen to the following dialogues and fill in the reservation slip below.

Golden Palace Restaurant		Table Reservation		
	Guest's Name	No. of People	Time	Private Room
1st Guest				
2nd Guest				
3rd Guest				

Useful Expressions

Welcome to Golden Palace.
Do you **have a reservation**, madam?
Please wait a minute. Yes, here it is, 5:00 p.m., Summer Hall.
It's on the first floor. Please **follow** me.
The private room **will be ready** at 6:30 p.m., as you reserved.
We **were expecting** you, Mr Black. This way, please.

Practice:

Now please discuss with your partner and answer the following question: "How do you serve the reserved guests?"

Serving Non-reserved Guests

Now you will listen to the following dialogues between a host and a guest. Decide whether the statements are True or False.

Dialogue A:

a. The guest wants a table for eight in Silver Cloud Restaurant.

b. The guest doesn't have a reservation.

c. There is no table for eight available in the restaurant right now.

d. The guest agrees to wait for 25 minutes in the lounge.

Dialogue B:

a. The guest wants a table for two.

b. The guest has a reservation.

c. There is a table for the guest in the restaurant.

d. The guest prefers the table near the window.

Useful Expressions

How many people, please?
I'm sorry. We **don't have** a table for nine available **right now**.
There will be one after 15 minutes, do you **mind waiting in the lounge**?
How about the table **near that window**?
We will **seat you** when we have a table.

Practice:

Now please discuss with your partner and answer the following question: "What can we say when we ask a guest for the reservation?"

Changing the Table

Please complete the conversation by filling in the missing words and expressions as you listen to the dialogue.

(H= Host, G=Guest)

H: Good evening, sir and madam. How many people, please?

G: Two. And I _____ yesterday. I reserved _____ near the window under the name of Thomas.

H: Please wait for a minute, sir. Let me _____… yes, Mr Thomas, a table for two. Please follow me.

G: Thank you.

H: Here it is.

G: Oh, it looks pretty narrow here ___ _____. I don't think it's suitable for us. Can we _____?

H: Well, if you don't like this one, where would you like to sit, sir?

G: Can we change our table to this one? It's much more spacious here.

H: I'm sorry, sir. The window tables _____. How about the table over there? It's further back but spacious. And you can still enjoy the view of the lake.

G: Ok. That's fine.

H: This way, please. _____, sir and madam.

G: Thank you. It's much better here and it makes us more relax. We can still _____ though it's a little bit further from the window. That's OK.

H: I'm so glad you like it. Please wait for a minute, the waiter _____ right away.

G: Thank you.

Useful Expressions

Well, if you don't like this one, **wherewould you like** to sit, sir?

I'm sorry, sir. The window tables **have all been taken**.

How about the table over there?

It's **further back but spacious**.

You can **still** enjoy the view of the lake.

Please wait for a minute, the waiter will be with you **right away**.

Practice:

For what reasons does a guest usually change the table in a restaurant?

Vocabulary

expect	[ɪk'spekt]	v.	期望，期盼
hall	[hɔ:l]	n.	大厅
impression	[ɪm'preʃn]	n.	印象，感觉
narrow	['nærəʊ]	adj.	狭窄的
patron	['peɪtrən]	n.	老主顾，顾客
redundant	[rɪ'dʌndənt]	adj.	多余的
spacious	['speɪʃəs]	adj.	宽敞的
suitable	['su:təbl]	adj.	合适的，适当的
typical	['tɪpɪkl]	adj.	典型的，特别的，有代表性的
tulip	['tju:lɪp]	n.	郁金香，郁金香形状的酒杯

a party of nine	一行九人
enjoy the view of	欣赏……的景色
in the name of	以……的名义
leave a good impression	留下一个好印象
private room	包厢
show ... up	领……上楼

Exercises

I. Please translate the following sentences:

1. 请稍等……是的，找到了，晚上七点，608包厢。
2. 就像您预订的，您的餐位在下午六点钟会准备好。

3. 那边的桌子怎么样？位置有点靠后，但是很宽敞。
4. 先生，如果您不喜欢这个座位，您想坐在哪里呢？
5. 请稍等，服务员马上就来为您服务。
6. Welcome to our restaurant. Do you have a reservation?
7. We were expecting you, Mrs Rice. This way, please.
8. I'm sorry. We don't have a table for nine available right now.
9. There will be one available in 20 minutes. Do you mind waiting in the lounge? We will seat you when we have a table.
10. I'm sorry, sir. The window tables have all been taken.

II. Role-play: Suppose you are working at a Japanese restaurant called Teriyaki Restaurant. Please work with your partner. Use the information of the table reservation record and try to make up a dialogue on welcoming the guests in the restaurant.

III. Please read the following materials about how to greet and seat guests. Then discuss with your classmates and answer the following questions.

The person who greets guests is a Host or Hostess. They welcome and escort our guests to their table. They set the mood for the restaurant.

1. Keep track of each station. Make a chart of each server's station, and what tables are in it (also learn the table layout by heart). Keep note of how many people are in a party and what table they are at. Also keep note of who is still there so that servers do not become overwhelmed.

2. Be aware as guests approach the restaurant. If you are busy with another guest, acknowledge the guest by saying, "I will be right with you," make eye contact, or a simple hand gesture also works.

3. Greet them with a smile and welcome them to the restaurant . Remember, you are the first chance for the restaurant to make a good impression, and set them at ease.

4. Find out how many people are dining. If there is a wait, make sure to get everyone's name right away so they do not feel ignored. Avoid giving them a specific time frame. Explain that we currently have a short wait, and that there should be a table ready momentarily, or we are currently getting tables cleared and set. NEVER say 5~10 minutes. Guests are generally impatient, and will find

somewhere else to dine.

Questions:

a. In order to keep good track of your service, what should you write in your notebook?

b. If there are many guests in your restaurant at the same time and you cannot serve them at the same time, what will you say and what will you do to them?

c. What will you do to welcome the guest to your restaurant?

d. What will you do if there is a wait in your restaurant right now?

How to be a great waiter/waitress in a restaurant?

1. Keep track of each station. Make a chart of each server's station, and what tables are in it (also learn the table layout by heart). Review all reservations for your shift, and assign suitable tables for each. Keep note of how many people are in a party, what time they arrived, and what table they are at. Also keep note of who is still there so that servers do not become overwhelmed.

2. Be aware as guests approach the restaurant. If you are busy with another guest, acknowledge the guest by saying, "I will be right with you," make eye contact, or a simple hand gesture also works.

3. Greet them with a smile and welcome them to the restaurant. Remember, you are the first and last chance for the restaurant to make a good impression, and set them at ease.

4. Find out how many people are dining. If there is a wait make sure to get everyone's name right away so they do not feel ignored. Guests will normally ask for a time frame. Never try to give a specific time. Tell them an "estimated" time. Look at the wait list and add 5 minutes for each party of the same size. If 6 parties of 2 are on the list, the estimated wait time would be 30 minutes for another party of 2. Guests are generally impatient, and will find somewhere else to dine.

5. After greeting the guests, look at the SIZE of the largest member of the party and assign the seating with that in mind. DON'T put them in a small booth! Also, a guest that has trouble walking should be given a seat as close to the hostess station as possible.

6. When the guest sits down, place a menu for each of them by the place setting, or hand the menu to the guest. Don't just throw menus on the table and leave without saying anything.

7. Be prepared to get some things for guests, water refills, utensils, napkins, or carryout boxes. If a guest does ask for something else, inform the guest that you will let his / her server know.

Scene Two — Taking Orders

One of the key expressions of a customer's experience in a restaurant is the level of service offered by the waiters or waitresses. If you are a waiter or a waitress, your primary responsibility is to ensure that all your guests are happy and their needs are met. You must also have a pleasant disposition and possess the flexibility to respond to a variety of demands from your guests. However, your most important duty is to ensure that you accurately take your guest's order so he receives the dish exactly the way he likes. When taking an order for any meal, the most important thing is to be sure that you have recorded the information correctly. You can also suggest specific dishes or specials to help the guest decide what to order. Taking an order is not as easy as one might think. It is imperative that you first know what you are doing.

In this unit, you will learn:

Western Food

Chinese Food

Part 3　Food & Beverage Department　餐饮服务英语 | 69

Buffet

Activities

Western Food

Listen to the dialogue and answer the following questions:

a. What does the waiter say when he presents the menu to the guest?

b. What dishes does the guest order?

c. What special requests does the guest ask about the main course?

d. What dessert and drink does the guest order?

e. What does the waiter say after taking the order?

Useful Expressions

Here is the menu.

I will be **right back to take your order**.

Excuse me, sir. **May I take your order,** now?

And do you want French fries or a **baked potato with the steak**?

 And for your dessert?

Would you like something **to drink with your meal**?

Your dish **will be ready soon**.

Practice:

Now please go through the dialogue again with your partner and discuss about the components of the western food.

Chinese Food

Now you will listen to a dialogue between a waiter and a guest. Decide whether the statements are True or False.

a. The guests would like to have Jasmine Tea to start with.

b. The guests like oily and spicy food the most.
c. "Steamed prawn with garlic sauce" is the chef's special today.
d. "Steamed pork ribs with rice powder" has two choices: small with 4 pieces and large with 6 pieces.
e. There are many kinds of soup in the restaurant, including ham and white gourd soup, tomato and egg soup, seaweed egg soup, etc.
f. The guests ordered five dishes totally.

Useful Expressions

Would anyone like a drink to **start with**?
We would like something delicious in **typical** Chinese style.
Which dishes do you prefer, **light, heavy, sweet or spicy**?
It's very tasty and it's our **chef's specialty** today.
The fresh prawns **are steamed with** garlic, soy sauce, white pepper, sesame oil and so on.
We **have** ham and white gourd soup, tomato and egg soup, seaweed egg soup, and so on.
What would you like to **go with** your dishes, fried rice, noodles, or steamed bread?
The dishes will **come out** in about 15 minutes.

Practice:

There are Eight Culinary Cuisines in China, they are Guangdong Cuisine, Sichuan Cuisine, Shandong Cuisine, Fujian Cuisine, Jiangsu Cuisine, Hunan Cuisine, Anhui Cuisine, and Zhejiang Cuisine. Please match the names with the dishes, and try to point out what cuisine it belongs to.

Dongpo Pork, Buddha Jumping Wall, Stewed Turtle with Ham, Four Joy Meatballs, Sweet and Sour Mandarin Fish, Hot Pot, Dry-Fried Beef and Noodles, Spicy Chicken

1. _____ 2. _____ 3. _____ 4. _____

5. _____ 6. _____ 7. _____ 8. _____

Buffet

Please complete the conversation by filling in the missing words and expressions as you listen to the dialogue.
(W= Waiter, G=Guest)

W: Good evening, sir and madam. How many people, please?

G: Well, _____. Do you have buffet in your restaurant?

W: Yes, sir. We have a buffet. You can have all you want for _____.

G: Do you have seafood for buffet?

W: Yes. We have a good selection of _____, _____, _____ and _____.

G: What drinks do you have?

W: We serve various kinds of soft drinks, such as _____, _____, _____, _____ and _____. We also serve several simple wines, like beer or red wine.

G: Great. We would like to have buffet here.

W: Certainly, sir. Would you like to sit here by the window?

G: Perfect. Thank you.

W: By the way, _____ and _____ are on the main buffet table over there, and the drinks are by the wall. Please help yourself.

G: Thank you!

Useful Expressions

Yes, sir. We **have** a buffet.
You can have **all you want** for 138 yuan.
We have **a good selection of** seafood, meat, dim sum and vegetables.
We serve **various kinds** of soft drinks, such as …
We also **serve** beer or simple red wine.
Silverware and dishes are on the **main buffet table** over there.
The drinks are **by the wall**.
Please **help yourself**.

Practice:

Buffet is also called self service and is normally used in banquet functions and in some restaurants. Food is attractively arranged on a long table, from appetizers to desserts. Instead of the waiter serving the guests, the guests go to the buffet table to pick up plates and serve themselves of their own choice. Please discuss with your partner and try to answer the question:

What are the advantages and disadvantages of having buffet?

Vocabulary

bake	[beɪk]	n.	烤，烘烤食品；
		v.	烤，烘焙
garlic	[ˈgɑːlɪk]	n.	大蒜
gourd	[gʊəd]	n.	葫芦，瓜
ham	[hæm]	n.	火腿
jasmine	[ˈdʒæzmɪn]	n.	茉莉，茉莉香料
juice	[dʒuːs]	n.	果汁
lemonade	[ˌleməˈneɪd]	n.	柠檬汁，柠檬饮料
lettuce	[ˈletɪs]	n.	生菜，莴苣
mushroom	[ˈmʌʃrʊm]	n.	蘑菇
oily	[ˈɔɪli]	adj.	油腻的，油多的
onion	[ˈʌnjən]	n.	洋葱
oyster	[ˈɔɪstə(r)]	n.	生蚝，牡蛎
pork	[pɔːk]	n.	猪肉
powder	[ˈpaʊdə(r)]	n.	粉，粉末状
prawn	[prɔːn]	n.	对虾，明虾
rib	[rɪb]	n.	肋骨
turtle	[ˈtɜːtl]	n.	龟，龟鳖
sauce	[sɔːs]	n.	酱汁，调味汁
sesame	[ˈsesəmi]	n.	芝麻
seaweed	[ˈsiːwiːd]	n.	海带，海藻
specialty	[ˈspeʃəlti]	n.	特色菜；
		adj.	特色的
spicy	[ˈspaɪsi]	adj.	辛辣的，香的
starter	[ˈstɑːtə(r)]	n.	开胃菜，开胃小吃
steam	[stiːm]	v.	蒸，煮
tableware	[ˈteɪblweə(r)]	n.	餐具，食具
French fries			炸薯条
ham and white gourd			冬瓜火腿汤
hot pot			火锅
ice cream			冰激凌
lettuce with oyster sauce			蚝油生菜
main course			主菜
soy sauce			酱油
steamed bread			馒头
steamed pork ribs with rice powder			粉蒸排骨
steamed prawn with garlic sauce			蒜茸蒸虾

Exercises

I. Please translate the following sentences:
1. 这是菜单。我马上过来为您点菜。
2. 您是想要薯条还是意大利面（spaghetti）来搭配牛排呢？
3. 您喜欢哪种口味的菜，清淡的，口味重的，偏甜的还是偏辣的？
4. 我们有各种海鲜、肉类、点心和蔬菜提供。
5. 餐具和餐碟就在那边的自助餐台上，请自行取用。
6. Would you like something to drink with your meal?
7. We would like something delicious in the typical Chinese style.
8. We have ham and white gourd soup, tomato and egg soup, seaweed egg soup, and so on.
9. What would you like to go with your dishes, fried rice, noodles, or dumplings?
10. Yes, sir. We have a buffet. You can have all you want for 138 yuan.

II. Role-play: Work in pairs. Student A is a waiter working in a western restaurant. Student B is a guest having dinner in the restaurant. Try to make up a dialogue on taking orders.

III. Please read the following materials about how to take orders for guests. Then discuss with your classmates and decide whether the following statements are true or false.

How to take guest orders in restaurants?

Every food and beverage service staff should have good command over order taking to ensure that each guest gets proper food he ordered and importantly in right sequence.

Step one: Give time to guests after their arrival to feel comfortable with the environment.

Step two: Greet the guests at the table with a smile as you make eye contact with each of them. State the specials of the day and make several recommendations. Ask if anyone has questions about an item on the menu.

Step three: Take the first order from the female guests, if applicable. If there are no women at the table, take the order based on your restaurant's sequential system or from the male guest who seems most ready to order. If your customer is trying to decide among several menu items, provide assistance by explaining how each dish is prepared.

Step four: Repeat the order back to every guest to ensure it is accurate. If someone orders a dish that can be prepared in several different ways — such as a steak — ask how the guest would like the item to be cooked. Repeating the order also allows you to ensure that you match each guest with the proper order.

Step five: Ask the diners if they would like to add anything to the order. Thank everyone, collect the menus and state that the meal will arrive shortly.

Statements:

a. Come to the guest to take order immediately after he arrives.

b. It's very important to greet the guests with body gestures, like eye contact or a smile.

c. There's no need to ask the guest whether he has questions about an item on the menu.

d. Try to take the first order from the female guests, if applicable.

e. Don't forget to repeat the order back to make a confirmation before you leave the table, especially the dish which can be cooked in several ways.

f. It doesn't matter if you forget to take the menu and leave it on the table. Just go back and ask the guest for it.

Do you know how to introduce the Chinese food?

Chinese cuisine includes styles originating from the diverse regions of China, as well as from Chinese people in other parts of the world. The history of Chinese cuisine in China stretches back for thousands of years and has changed from period to period and in each region according to climate, imperial fashions, and local preferences. Over time, techniques and ingredients from the cuisines of other cultures were integrated into the cuisine of the Chinese people due both to imperial expansion and from the trade with nearby regions in pre-modern times, and from Europe and the New World in the modern period. In addition, dairy is rarely—if ever—used in any recipes in the style.

According to food critic Bonny Wolf, Chinese cuisine is one of the "Three Grand Cuisines" in the world, together with the French and Turkish cuisines.

The "Eight Culinary Cuisines" of China are Anhui, Cantonese, Fujian, Hunan, Jiangsu, Shandong, Sichuan, and Zhejiang cuisines.

Prominent styles of Chinese cuisine outside China include Singaporean, Malaysian, Indonesian, Indian and American, but there is Chinese cuisine wherever Chinese people are found. The staple foods of Chinese cooking include rice, noodles, vegetables, and sauces and seasonings.

Scene Three Serving Dishes

The secret of a food and beverage service operation's success in a hotel is that everyone works together as a team. Waiters and waitresses are considered to be a vital part of a service delivery system. In order to make each guest's dining experience exactly what he or she wants it to be and exceed guest's expectations whenever possible, waiters and waitresses are expected to serve guests while keeping politeness, organization and efficiency standards. Since high guest satisfaction often leads to higher tips and return customers, it's important for servers to learn the fundamentals of restaurant food service. Proper food serving in a formal setting requires the server to follow several rules, including serving plates of food from the right, carrying plates properly and removing food from the left.

In this unit, you will learn:

Slow In Serving

Serving Wrong Dish

Special Service

Activities

Slow In Serving

Listen to the dialogue and complete the information:

a. The guests have been waiting for _____ minutes until now.
b. The waiter says he will check the order with _____.
c. The guests are in a hurry to attend a meeting in _____ minutes.
d. The waiter expresses an apology for the delay by saying _____.
e. The waiter gives extra _____ to the guests to say sorry.

Useful Expressions

I'm **very sorry**, madam.
I **understand**, madam.
Just a moment, please.
I will **check your order with the chef** right now.
Sorry to **have kept you waiting**, madam.
We are very sorry **for the delay**.

They're **free of charge**.
Please **enjoy your lunch**.

Practice:

Guests usually give the waiter a hard time about the food taking too long. Many of them are just up and leaving. Please discuss with your classmates about how to fix the problem of slowness.

Serving Wrong Dish

Please listen to the dialogues and decide whether the following statements are true or false.

Dialogue A:

a. The guest asks the waiter to come because he wants to order dish.

b. The guest orders fried rice, but gets shrimp noodles.

c. The waiter doesn't take the dish away.

d. The waiter apologizes to the guest.

Dialogue B:

a. The guest orders a spiced spring chicken in chili.

b. The dish will be ready in about 20 minutes.

c. The waiter will check the order with chef soon.

d. The guest gets a complementary drink but pays for the steamed chicken with rice flour.

Useful Expressions

There **must have been** some mistake.
I **do apologize for** giving you the wrong dish.
Your dish **will be ready** in about 15 minutes.
I will **cross it off your bill**.
And here is the **complementary drink** for you while waiting.
I'm very sorry **for the mistake**.
I **assure you** it won't happen again.

Practice:

Now please discuss with your partner and talk about how to deal with the problem of serving the wrong dish to the guests.

- Be genuine:

- Be brief:
  _____

- Be genuine:
  _____

Special Service

Please complete the conversation by filling in the missing words and expressions as you listen to the dialogue.

(W= Waiter, G=Guest)

W: Excuse me, sir. _____?

G: Yes, please.

W: Here are your dishes. This one is tomato fish pieces, and this one is grilled pigeon.

G: They smell so good. Thank you.

W: You are welcome, sir. Does the high chair _____?

G: Yes, it's just suitable for him. Thank you.

W: Great, if you need any help, please let me know.

G: Sure, thanks!

(two minutes later …)

W: Excuse me, sir. _____. It's very hot, please take care.

G: Thank you.

W: How do you like the food?

G: Well, it's very _____.

W: I'm so happy to hear that. By the way, here is the flatware for your daughter, _____. They are smaller, easier and safer for your child to cut and eat the food. And this _____ is for your baby son.

G: Wow, that's very kind of you. Thank you so much, they are so happy to have the dinner here!

W: It's my pleasure. Shall I change this plate to _____?

G: Sure, go ahead.

W: Thank you, sir. _____?

G: No, everything is perfect. Thank you!

W: You are welcome, sir. Wish you have a good time with your family!

Useful Expressions

If you need any help, please **let me know**.

It's very hot, please **take care**.

How do you like the food?

Here is the flatware for your daughter.

They are smaller, easier and safer **for your child** to cut and eat the food.

Shall I change this plate to a smaller one?

Wish you have a good time with your family!

Practice:

Now please discuss with your partner about the possible special requirements from different guests. Please match the guests with their possible needs.

A. a vegetarian guest
B. a guest with a baby
C. a guest with gluten allergies
D. a guest who is on diet
E. a guest who wants to save time
F. a Muslim guest

1. healthy foods that are low in fat and calories
2. a meal without meat
3. Muslim food
4. gluten-free food
5. high chair
6. fast food

Vocabulary

allergy	[ˈælədʒi]	n.	过敏反应
apologize	[əˈpɒlədʒaɪz]	v.	道歉，认错
assure	[əˈʃʊə(r)]	v.	保证，使……确信
calorie	[ˈkæləri]	n.	卡路里（热量单位）
cause	[kɔːz]	n.	原因，理由；
		v.	导致，引起
chili	[ˈtʃɪli]	n.	红辣椒
complimentary	[ˌkɒmplɪˈmentri]	adj.	赠送的
flatware	[ˈflætweə(r)]	n.	扁平的餐具（尤指刀，叉，匙等）
gluten	[ˈɡluːtn]	n.	面筋，麸质
grilled	[ɡrɪld]	adj.	烤的，烤过的
Muslim	[ˈmʊzlɪm]	n.	穆斯林，伊斯兰信徒；
		adj.	穆斯林的
noodle	[ˈnuːdl]	n.	面条
pigeon	[ˈpɪdʒɪn]	n.	鸽子
safe	[seɪf]	adj.	安全的，保险的
soda	[ˈsəʊdə]	n.	苏打水，汽水
toy	[tɔɪ]	n.	玩具
check the order			检查点菜单
cross ... off			从（账单）上划掉
free of charge			免费
fried rice			炒饭
high chair			儿童椅
low in fat and calories			脂肪和热量较低的

on diet	减肥
on the house	免费
steamed chicken with rice flour	粉蒸鸡
Spiced Spring Chicken in Chili	炸子鸡
3-piece child set	儿童三件餐具套装
tomato fish pieces	番茄鱼片

Exercises

I. Please translate the following sentences:
1. 这是给您的两份苏打饮料，都是免费的，祝您午餐愉快！
2. 非常抱歉给您上错菜了，我马上就去和厨师核对一下点菜单，把您的菜尽快给您端来。
3. 很抱歉让您久等了。您的菜 15 分钟之后就会准备好。
4. 我为我们的错误向您道歉。我保证以后不会发生这样的事了。
5. 这是提供给您女儿的餐具，儿童三件餐具套装。希望您和您的家人用餐愉快！
6. I'm awfully sorry, sir. There must have been some mistake.
7. Great, if you need any help, please let me know.
8. If you don't mind, please try this one. I will cross it off your bill.
9. Here is the complementary drink for you while waiting.
10. Shall I change this plate to a smaller one?

II. Role-play: Work in pairs. Student A has ordered a crispy pepper duck, but gets a boiled salted duck. Student B is apologizing to the guest and solving the mistake.

III. Please read the following materials about how to serve food for guests. Then discuss with your classmates and decide whether the following statements are T (true) or F (false).

When you are serving plates of food, carry one in each hand. Stand at the left of the person you are serving, place in front of her the plate you are holding in your left hand. Then transfer to your left hand the plate you are holding in your right hand, move to the next person, and serve her in the same manner.

When you pass food to a person at the table, offer it at her left, low enough so she can reach it conveniently with her right hand. Then move to the next person at the first person's right.

When you remove soiled dishes, stand at the left of the person and take the plate in your left hand. Transfer the plate to your right hand, leaving your left hand free to remove the next plate.

If a guest requests more water, fill her glass or goblet without removing it from the table. Hold the pitcher of water in the right hand and a folded napkin in the left hand to catch any water that drips as the glass is being refilled. As a matter of routine, water glasses or goblets are refilled after the main course plates are removed, and before dessert is served.

Statements:

a. When you are serving plates of food, carry one in each hand. Stand at the right of the person you are serving, place in front of her the plate you are holding in your left hand.

b. When you pass food to a person at the table, offer it at her left.

c. When you remove soiled dishes, stand at the right of the person and take the plate in your left hand.

d. If a guest requests more water, you should take the glass away, fill the guest's glass and give it back to the guest.

Rules for Serving Food

Serving food

Carry plates one in each hand so that fingers do not touch the top of the plate, and be sure to set the left plate down first. Plates of food are served from the right, while platters of food and pans are served from the left. When serving food from a tray, offer it to the guest from the left hand, bending down so that they can easily serve themselves from the tray. Do not reach across the guests lap or table space at any time while serving.

Refilling and serving drinks

Place and remove beverages with the right hand while standing on the guest's left. Refill glasses from the left without disturbing or lifting the glass. Instead, use a pitcher and hold a folded napkin at the edge to catch any spilled liquids.

Removing dishes

Remove empty dishes at the end of each meal or course, not as they are emptied, unless performing another function, such as filling a beverage. Transfer plates to the left hand from the right, and if necessary, stack them on the hand rather than on the table. Remove serving dishes first, then plates and utensils and then glasses.

Scene Four — Bar Service

Bar Service is an important hotel service that serves alcoholic beverages, such as beer, wine, liquor, cocktails, and other beverages like mineral water and soft drinks and often sells snack foods, like chips or peanuts, for consumption on premises. Good service includes how bartenders interact with customers when things are going well, as well as how bartenders handle difficult situations. The best bartenders develop customer service relationships with bar guests who feel at home while visiting the bar and having a couple of drinks or a fun night out. Also, bartenders may have to make arrangements for glasses, napkins, setups, and other items necessary for proper bar functioning.

In this unit, you will learn:

Serving Wines

Communicating With Guests

Conflict Resolution

Activities

Serving Wine

Now you will listen to a dialogue. Decide whether the statements are True or False.

a. There are many kinds of alcohol served in the bar, such as brandy, whiskey, gin, vodka and so on.

b. One of the guests would like to have a Scottish brandy.

c. The other guests want to have a glass of stout.

d. The guests also want to have pretzels as their snacks.

e. The guests will pay in cash right now.

Useful Expressions

We serve brandy, whiskey, gin, vodka and so on. **What would you like**?

With soda or water?

We have bottled beer, stout and draught beer.

I will be **right back** with your drinks.

Would you like **anything else**?

How about snacks, **such as** potato chips or pretzels?

You may **sign the bill** since you are staying at our hotel.

Practice:

Now please discuss with your partner and match the following bar snacks with their pictures.

| pretzel | chicken wings | potato chips | fried peanuts |
| pop corn | onion rings | | |

English For Hotel Staff
Developing Skills
酒店实用英语（灵活应用篇）

a. _____ b. _____ c. _____

d. _____ e. _____ f. _____

Communicating With Guests

Listen to the dialogue and answer the following questions:

a. Does the guest feel happy in the bar?

b. What is the new style of cocktail recommended by the bartender?

c. How long does the bartender work in the bar?

d. Where is the guest from?

e. What questions does the bartender ask to the guest?

Useful Expressions

Did you **enjoy your drink**, sir?

Would you like to **try another** kind of our new style?

How long have you been working here?

I enjoy working here **because** I can meet different people and make friends with them.

Where are you from?

Do you **like the city**?

Are you here **on vocation** or **business**?

Practice:

Suppose you are working at a bar in the hotel. What topics are easier for you to start a talk with your guests?

Conflict Resolution

Please complete the conversation by filling in the missing words and expressions as you listen to the dialogue.

(B= Bartender, G=Guest)

B: Good evening, sir. How many people, please?

G: Well, _____.

B: Would you like a table for five?

G: Yes.

B: Follow me, please. Will this table do?

G: It's fine. Do you have _____?

B: Yes. We have Heineken, Budweiser and Carlsberg. What would you like?

G: Please give us _____.

B: Certainly, sir. Anything else?

G: No, thanks.

(About an hour later, two of the guests get drunk. One of them begins to shout and the other one begins to sing loudly …)

B: Excuse me, sir. _____? Do you need some tea or water now? I think your friends may need it.

G: Sorry to disturb other guests here. Yes, _____.

B: I will come with the tea right now. Maybe your friends will feel better when _____, sir. It's very stuffy and noisy here.

G: Yeah, I understand. Sorry.

Useful Expressions

Would you like **a table for five**?

Excuse me, sir. Is everything **all right**?

Do you need some tea or water **now**? I think your friends **may need** it.

Maybe your friends will feel better when they have **more fresh air**, sir.

It's very **stuffy** and **noisy** here.

Practice:

Now please discuss with your partner: "How to handle the drunk guests?"

Vocabulary

ancient	[ˈeɪnʃənt]	adj.	古老的，古代的
brilliant	[ˈbrɪliənt]	adj.	美好的，才华横溢的
capital	[ˈkæpɪtl]	n.	首都
cocktail	[ˈkɒkteɪl]	n.	鸡尾酒
cultural	[ˈkʌltʃərəl]	adj.	文化的
disturb	[dɪˈstɜːb]	v.	打扰
double	[ˈdʌbl]	adj.	双倍的，双份的

draught	[drɑːft]	adj.	一口之量，一饮
dynasty	['dɪnəsti]	n.	朝代，王朝
gin	[dʒɪn]	n.	杜松子酒
heritage	['herɪtɪdʒ]	n.	遗产，文化遗产
import	['ɪmpɔːt]	v.	进口
lychee	['lɪtʃi]	n.	荔枝
martini	[mɑːˈtiːni]	n.	马丁尼酒
pretzel	['pretsl]	n.	椒盐脆饼
Seattle	[sɪˈætl]	n.	西雅图（美国城市名称）
snack	[snæk]	n.	快餐
stout	[staʊt]	n.	烈性黑啤酒
stuffy	['stʌfi]	adj.	闷热的，不通气的

Budweiser	百威啤酒
Carlsberg	嘉士伯啤酒
Confucius Temple	夫子庙
Dr. Sun Yat-sen's Mausoleum	中山陵
draught beer	生啤酒
Heineken	喜力啤酒
on the rocks	加冰块
potato chips	薯条
Purple Mountain	紫金山
Qinhuai River	秦淮河
Scottish gin	苏格兰杜松子酒

Exercises

I. Please translate the following sentences:

1. 由于您在酒店住宿，只要签单就可以了。酒店会在您离开的时候一并结账。
2. 我们有白兰地，威士忌，杜松子酒，伏特加等。您想要哪一种？
3. 您还需要什么吗？来点小吃怎么样，比如薯条或者椒盐卷饼？
4. 您是在这里度假还是出差呢？
5. 您的朋友呼吸更多的新鲜空气可能会好些。这里又闷又吵。
6. Do you need some tea or water now? I think your friends may need it.
7. Would you like to try another kind of our new style?
8. I enjoy working here because I can meet different people and make friends with them.

9. How long have you been working here?
10. Excuse me, sir. Is everything all right?

II. Role-play: Work in pairs. Student A is a bartender working in the Silver Bar. Student B is a guest having the drinks in the bar. Try to make up a dialogue on serving wines according to the following menu.

- Please read the following materials about how to create a conversation between a bartender and his guests. Then discuss with your classmates and decide whether the following statements are true or false.

When making conversations with your guests, it is important to remember to keep it quick as well as neutral. As busy as you may be with other customers, you'll probably only get in a few sentences at a time.

But you should know that there are a few subjects that you don't want to bring up, especially as a bartender. In order to keep the peace at your bar or table, don't talk about politics or religion. Religion and politics are topics that simply don't mix well with alcohol, at least not at a public bar. People tend to feel overly passionate about these subjects, and the alcohol in their systems only intensifies this affect.

And, at a bar or restaurant, you will hardly ever go wrong if you bring up the topics of Sports or News (remember, though, if you decide to talk about news, make it current events, not politics!) What if you are not a sports or news expert? Don't worry, you don't have to be. You have all you need right there at the restaurant or bar. Nine times out of ten, there is a newspaper around somewhere. All you have to do is browse the headlines that catch your eyes the most. Then, when you see the opportunity, ask your customers if they have heard about that story or ball game. They will probably end up buying even more drinks and food if this type of fun conversation gets good!

Also, there is nothing wrong with telling a joke or two every now and then. If you tell a joke, be sure it is tasteful and doesn't offend anyone.

Statements:

a. When starting a conversation with your guests, it's very important to keep it quick and neutral.

b. As a wonderful bartender, you should greet each guest by talking a lot in the bar.

c. There are two sensitive topics between the bartender and the guests: religion and politics.

d. In order to serve the guests better, a bartender benefits from being a sports or news expert.

e. Browsing the headlines of the newspaper around you can help you to create a talk with your guests whenever there is an opportunity.

f. It's ok for a bartender to tell a joke to the guests, but remember to make sure the joke should be inoffensive.

Different Types of Bar Service

Depending on your budget and the nature of your party, you may want to tailor the bar service. Some options include:

Premium Bar

A premium bar serves alcohol listed as the highest quality, such as imported liquor, beer and wine. This is the most elaborate arrangement, and includes all the set ups.

Standard Bar

A standard bar may exclude premium liquor but includes local liquor, beer, wine, and set ups.

Wine and Beer

This type of bar service offers beer or wine only. The brands are up to the host.

Wine Tasting

A wine tasting bar is usually part of a theme. The wines are specially selected, and guests are invited to offer their opinions. This is typically an open bar situation.

Open Bar

An open bar can be premium or standard, wine or beer only, but guests do not pay for their liquor. Bartender rates may be a little higher since guests are not expected to offer gratuities.

Cash Bar

A cash bar can be any combination listed here, but the guests are expected to pay for their beverages. The bartender's fee may be a little less than a cash bar since guests usually tip for the service.

Hiring a bar service for a party adds to the ambience of a party or reception. Using a service makes hosting easier, and frees everyone to enjoy guests and the conviviality of the evening.

Scene Five — Room Service

Room service or "in-room dining" is a hotel service enabling guests to choose menu items for delivery to their hotel room for consumption there, and served by staff. A room service server may have many different responsibilities. The server usually reports to a room service manager while working. He is expected to restock items, take orders, and deliver those orders to each room at a hotel or lodge. The server may also have to help with other areas of the hotel when room service orders are slow. The hotel guests will call the room service number to place an order. The server will take the food order and hand it off to the kitchen. After the kitchen staff prepares the food, the server will then place it on the cart and deliver the order to the correct room.

In this unit, you will learn:

Doorknob Menu

Ordering Meals

Serving Meals

Activities

Doorknob Menu

listen to the dialogue and answer the following questions:

a. What are the guest's name and room number?

b. Room service can come in three different ways in this hotel. What are they?

c. What food is usually offered on the Door Knob Menu?

d. How to use the Door Knob Menu?

e. What time does the hotel usually serve breakfast?

Useful Expressions

You can **simply press** "0" or Service Express on your telephone for all of your room service needs.

You can **use** our Breakfast Door Knob Menu.

The menu offers **many dining choices** from breakfast selections, sandwiches, burgers, entrees to pizza served in your room.

It is **a convenient way** to order your breakfast in advance.

Just put it out on your doorknob **before you go to sleep**.

Your breakfast will **be delivered to** your room at your requested time.

Breakfast can be served **in your room** from 7:00 a.m. until 10:00 a.m.

Practice:

A room service menu usually lists a limited number of breakfast items and service times for selection by the guest. Do you know how does the doorknob menu work?

Part 3 Food & Beverage Department 餐饮服务英语 91

Ordering Meals

Please listen to a dialogue and fill in the missing information.

ROOM SERVICE RECORD	NO. OF PEOPLE: TWO
TIME: 11:40 A.M.	
FOOD	
DRINK	
GUEST'S NAME	
ROOM NUMBER	

Useful Expressions

Yes, everything is **on the menu**.

Would you like anything **to drink**?

What kind of coffee would you prefer, **caramel macchiato or vanilla latte**?

We **add** a 10 percent service charge.

Your meal will **be prepared** soon.

Practice:

Now please discuss with your partner and talk about how to provide the room service.

Serving Meals

Please complete the conversation by filling in the missing words and expressions as you listen to the dialogue.

(W= Waiter, G=Guest)

W: _____. May I come in?

G: Come in, please.

W: Good evening, Mr Bacon. Here is the dinner you ordered.

G: Thank you, _____, please.

W: Certainly, sir. Here is your _____, _____ and _____. Shall I pour you a glass of beer straight away, Mr Bacon?

G: No, thanks. I'll pour it myself in a minute.

W: Ok. Here is your bill. Would you please sign your name here?

G: No problem. _____.

W: Thank you, Mr Bacon. We will add the cost to your room bill. If you need anything else, _____. We are always at your service.

G: Thank you.

W: You are welcome. Have a pleasant evening!

Useful Expressions

Room service. **May I come in**?

Here is the dinner **you ordered**.

Shall I pour you a glass of beer **straight away**, Mr Bacon?

Here is your bill. Would you **please sign** your name here?

We will **add the cost to** your room bill.

If you need anything else, **please feel free to** call us.

We are **always at your service**.

Have a **pleasant evening**!

Practice:

Now please discuss with your partner and match the following terms of room service with their pictures.

| linens and napkins | flatware, dishware | glassware |
| room service cart | in-room dinning menu | |

a. _____ b. _____ c. _____

d. _____ e. _____ f. _____

Vocabulary

add	[æd]	v.	增加，补充
burger	['bɜːgə(r)]	n.	汉堡包
convenient	[kən'viːniənt]	adj.	方便的
deliver	[dɪ'lɪvə(r)]	v.	交付，递送
extra	['ekstrə]	adj.	额外的，附加的
grapefruit	['greɪpfruːt]	n.	葡萄柚，西柚
latte	['lɑːteɪ]	n.	拿铁咖啡
mix	[mɪks]	v.	混合，调配
offer	['ɒfə(r)]	v.	提供，给予
pizza	['piːtsə]	n.	比萨
pour	[pɔː(r)]	v.	倒出，斟
prepare	[prɪ'peə(r)]	v.	准备，配备
press	[pres]	v.	按，压
salmon	['sæmən]	n.	三文鱼，鲑鱼
tuna	['tjuːnə]	n.	金枪鱼
vanilla	[və'nɪlə]	n.	香草；
		adj.	香草味的

Caesar salad	恺撒沙拉
Caramel Macchiato	焦糖玛奇朵咖啡
Door Knob Menu	挂门餐牌
Penne Pasta	意大利通心粉
room service	房内送餐服务
Service Express	快速服务
smoked salmon	烟熏三文鱼
straight away	马上，立即

Exercises

I. Please translate the following sentences:

1. 房内送早餐的时间是上午7点到10点。
2. 您可以在电话上拨"0"号键或者快捷服务键，选择我们所有的房内送餐服务。
3. 菜单提供很多房内用餐选择，从早餐，三明治，汉堡，主菜到比萨，应有尽有。
4. 房内送餐服务，请问可以进来吗？

5. 如果您还需要其他服务，请随时打电话联系我们。
6. What kind of coffee would you prefer, caramel macchiato or vanilla latte?
7. Your meal will be prepared soon.
8. You can use our Breakfast Door Knob Menu. It is a convenient way to order your breakfast in advance.
9. Just put it out on your doorknob before you go to sleep.
10. Shall I pour you a glass of beer straight away, Mr Bacon?

II. Role-play: Work in pairs. Student A is calling for a room service and ordering the food from the following menu and asking the waiter questions about the selections. Student B is answering the phone politely and taking the food and drink order. Please remember to tell the guest how long it will take and how much it costs. Then Student B will bring the food to the guest's room.

Room Service Menu

Treat yourself. Just pick up the phone.

SALADS AND APPETIZERS

Chicken Noodle Soup
Caesar Salad
Smoked Salmon
Grilled Goat's Cheese

SANDWICH ISLAND

Ham and Cheese Sandwich
Turkey and Cheese Sandwich
Tuna Burger
Steak Sandwich

SNACKS

Buttered Popcorn
Salted Peanuts

WINES AND BEVERAGE

Heineken
Budweiser
Carlsberg
Juice (*Orange, Apple, Figs, Grapefruit*)
Milk Shake
Coffee

- Please read the following materials about how to serve a room service. Then discuss with your classmates and answer the following questions.

Once the order is delivered to the room, the room service server will go over the order with the hotel guest to be sure it is correct. The server will also take items off the cart and place them neatly on the room table. He is usually expected to be polite and build a good rapport with hotel guests. When guests are done with their food trays, the server is responsible for picking up the dirty dishes and bringing them back to the kitchen.

Room service employees are also expected to keep the hotel minibars and snack items stocked in each room. If a guest has a special request, the server may also have to fulfill those demands as well. The room service server can also help serve food in the hotel restaurant or bar when it is especially busy.

Since the room service server has so many duties, he often has to have prior experience to get a job in a hotel. Hotel employers look for people who have customer service skills or have had a job serving customers within the food industry. Servers should also be neat in appearance and have an enthusiastic attitude with the customers and the other hotel employees.

Questions:

a. Once the order is delivered to the room, what's the first thing the server should do?

b. What will the server do when guests are done with their food trays?

c. Will the room server still need to keep the hotel minibars and snack items stocked in each room?

d. What kind of people will be suitable for the job of room service?

Tips

How to Make the Most Out of Room Service?

Room service is one of the most attractive aspects of staying in a hotel, as having a hot, delectable meal delivered to your hotel room is private and enjoyable. This is especially true for those fatigued and drained travelers. While room service may be expensive depending on your budget, it gives you the opportunity to do things you won't normally do in your own home, such as watch television as you eat, or eat in bed, and leave your dirty dishes in the hallway for someone else to take care of.

With regard to the price you pay for room service, many people think that hotels overcharge. However, the price for the delivery of a meal to a room is actually comparable to running a restaurant that provides full service. This is ideal for those who are traveling for business and have no time to dine out. Regardless of your situation, you have the ability to make the best out of room service in your hotel room. Here's how!

Consider going to an area fast food place for at least one or two of your meals, depending on the length of your hotel stay. Many people are still feeling the effects of the economic downturn and need more mealtime dining options.

Be as calculating as possible, remembering to account for all charges that come with room service. In addition to the price of your food, hotels also add taxes, a delivery charge that is a lump sum that goes directly to the hotel, and a service charge that goes to the employee. Before you confirm your order, ask questions about your grand total and clarify whether or not gratuity is included in that total. Usually, gratuity on net food and beverage costs average 15% to 20%.

Last but not least, ask more questions as to what you should expect with room service in regards to your meal and estimated delivery time. If you are a picky eater, ask to speak to the kitchen directly. Ask for details regarding what comes with your meal, such as if sides and condiments are included or if your entrée is a la carte. Before hanging up, ask the employee to repeat your order. As far as expected delivery times go, expect at least a half-hour to forty-five minutes during peak times.

When you take these things into considerations, you can make your room service experience as five star as the hotel in which you are staying!

Other Services
其他服务英语

Part 4

Brainstorm

Please look at the picture of the Fitness Center in this hotel, and describe what the Fitness Center looks like. As a class, list words you used to describe the possible staff, services, amenities or facilities this hotel might have. Then discuss them with your groups. See which group has the largest vocabulary.

people, places, things, services…

Scene One

Conference Services

When the hotel hosts a conference, it's necessary to know the specific goals the clients require. Then the hotel will provide potential ideas, planning, reception and facilitation. The Director of Sales & Marketing will communicate with the clients confirming their requirements in order to provide correctly, such as appropriate conference halls, meeting and presentation equipment within budget, the right eating and drinking location, a suitable menu within the budget, the room types, transportation and preparation of the meeting. After negotiation, they need to prepare a contract. Both sides sign the formal agreement and should obey the agreement strictly. The shared goal is to make the meeting succeed and give the meeting attendees a professional and memorable experience.

In this unit, you will learn:

Introduction Of Facilities

Contract Negotiation

Conference Registration

Activities

Introduction Of Facilities

Listen to the dialogue about Conference Reservation and finish the information in the form below.

Conference Date :
Conference Name:
Number of Participants:
Conference Hall Booked:
Meeting Facilities:
Other requirements:
Contact Number of The Guest:

Useful Expressions

When will the conference be?
What kind of conference will you hold and **how many people will attend**, Mr. Washington?
The exact number of delegates has not **been finalized**.
We expect that 300 participants will attend the conference.
One seats 400 people; **the other can accommodate up to** 600 attendees.
What **meeting facilities** do you need?
We need a **multi-media projector**, and a **video-camera** in the large room, as well as a **multi-media projector** and a **flip chart** in each small room.

Practice:

Discuss what information we need to know when someone books conference rooms.

Contract Negotiation

Listen to a conversation of discussing terms. Please complete it by filling in the missing words and expressions as you listen to the dialogue.
Scene: Martin Washington comes to the hotel to discuss the terms with Susan, the convention service manager.

(M=Manager, C=Customer)

M: Pleased to meet you, Mr. Washington. I'm Susan. I've been expecting you.

C: Pleased to meet you, too, Susan. I'd like to _____

of the conference service with you.

M: Have you _____?

C: Yes, we have 350 attendees in all. I want to make some changes to what I told you about the conference halls last time. We'll need the large conference hall from _____, and 8 small meeting rooms from October 28 to 29. The facilities are the same.

M: OK. Would you like some rooms?

C: Yes, we'd like to reserve _____. And _____ for the V.I.Ps in all.

M: Could you show me _____ so that I can assign the proper rooms for them?

C: Here you are. Is there any discount for conference reservation?

M: Yes. I went to see the General Manager yesterday, and he agreed to _____ _____ for the whole package.

C: Thank you very much.

M: It's my pleasure. Could you tell me your _____ for the conference?

C: The suppers on the first day and the last day of the conference are _____ _____.The other meals are buffets.

M: OK. We have Burgundy and some famous Chinese wine, like Great Wall, Dynasty and Chateau Changyu-Castel. They taste good and _____.

C: Well, please provide some Burgundy and Great Wall for the banquet.

M: OK. I'll make the arrangement. Would you follow me to my office to _____ _____ please ?

C: Yeah. Thanks for your help.

Useful Expressions

I'd like to discuss some details of the conference service with you.

Have you finalized the number of participants?

Yes, **we'd like to reserve** 160 standard rooms. And 30 deluxe rooms for the V.I.Ps in all.

Could you show me a guest list so that I can **assign the proper rooms** for them?

Could you tell me your **catering requirements for the conference**?

The suppers **on the first day and the last day** of the conferenceare banquets with some wine.

I'll **make the arrangement.**

Would you follow me to my office to **sign the printed contract** please ?

Practice:

Discuss what services the hotel usually provides during a conference.

Part 4　Other Services　其他服务英语 | 101

Conference Registration

Listen to the dialogue about registering for a conference and answer the following questions:

a. Has the guest registered before the meeting?
b. Where does the attendee registering for the conference come from?
c. What does the receptionist give to Peter Donald?
d. What is there in the meeting packet?
e. Who is staying in the room next to Sophie Donald's?

Useful Expressions

Have you **pre-registered**?
Here is your **meeting badge and meeting packet**.
The packet contains a layout of the hotel, a map of downtown Shanghai, information about scenic spots and other related items.
We've put you in Room 1509. **Here is** your room card.
Amy will **show you to** your room, and she will **serve you during the conference**.

Practice:

Choose the right word or phrase to fill in each blank.

| register | badge | layout | scenic spot | related |

1. The Sun Yat-sen's Mausoleum area is a world-famous _____.
2. Being a Communist was a _____ of honor for thousands of trade union activists.
3. This boat has a good deck _____ making everything easy to operate.
4. A spokesman insisted the two events were "in no way _____."
5. Many students _____ for these courses to widen skills for use in their current job.

Vocabulary

academic	[ˌækəˈdemɪk]	adj.	学术的，学院的，文学的
assign	[əˈsaɪn]	v.	分配，分派
badge	[bædʒ]	n.	徽章
banquet	[ˈbæŋkwɪt]	n.	宴会
Burgundy	[ˈbɜːgəndi]	n.	勃艮第葡萄酒
consult	[kənˈsʌlt]	v.	咨询

delegate	['delɪgət]	n.	代表；
		vt.	委派代表
Dynasty	['dɪnəsti]	n.	王朝葡萄酒
finalize	['faɪnəlaɪz]	v.	使结束；把……最后定下来
interpreter	[ɪn'tɜ:prɪtə(r)]	n.	口译员
layout	['leɪaʊt]	n.	布局，设计，规划图
participant	[pɑ:'tɪsɪpənt]	n.	参加者
register	['redʒɪstə(r)]	v.	登记
seminar	['semɪnɑ:(r)]	n.	研讨班；培训会

catering requirement	餐饮要求
Chateau Changyu-Castel	张裕卡斯特
Convention Service	会议服务
flip chart	活动挂图板
Great Wall	长城葡萄酒
guest list	宾客名单
meeting badge	会议徽章
meeting facility	会议设备
meeting packet	会议袋
multi-media project	多媒体放映机
scenic spot	风景区，名胜
video-camera	摄像机

Exercises

I. Please translate the following sentences:

1. 早上好。我们想在你们酒店里举行会议，我可以和负责这项工作的人谈一谈吗？
2. 我们酒店的会议厅配备完善，可满足您的需求。
3. 请问有多少人参加会议？
4. 我想和您协商一下会议服务的一些细节。
5. 会议的第一天和最后一天的晚餐为宴会。
6. They also need some office support services, such as the telex, photocopying and secretarial services, and 20 laptop computers.
7. Can you send us a VIPs list so that we can assign the proper rooms for them?
8. Good morning, sir. Would you like to register for the conference?
9. Mr. Robinson, you've been arranged in Room 2312. This is a deluxe suite. Here is your key card. And here is your meeting badge and meeting packet.

10. Dr. Moran from Colombia University is coming to register for the conference. He has pre-registered.

II. Role-play: Perform booking the conference service on the phone in pairs according to the following two cards.

The Guest's Card

The goal: hold a meeting to launch the new products

The time: June 14

The size of the meeting room: About 200 square meters

Want to know the rate

The Manager's Card

Goal of the meeting

Time of the meeting

Size of the meeting room

The rate is 9 000 yuan for every 100 square meters

- The following is a list of conference facilities. Please find the items that match Chinese phrases in the table below.

A. earphone
B. microphone
C. loudspeaker
D. flip chart
E. white board
F. laser printer
G. laptop computer
H. audiovisual
I. slide projector
J. multimedia projector
K. film projector
L. television
M. video recorder

电影放映机（ ）	笔记本电脑（ ）	耳机（ ）
麦克风（ ）	视听设备（ ）	扩音器（ ）
幻灯片投影仪（ ）	活动挂图（ ）	电视机（ ）
录像机（ ）	白板（ ）	多媒体投影机（ ）
激光打印机（ ）		

Tips

How to specify the nature of the conference?

Once having a team you need to specify the actual nature of the conference. Try to provide answers to the following questions in order to determine the nature of the conference.

- Who is the conference going to address?
- Who is most likely to attend it?
- Which specific linguistics will be covered?
- Will it have a specific theme within the area?
- Is it going to be a regional or European conference?
- Where will it be held?
- How long should it last?
- What is the scope of the conference?

In order to be able to answer these questions you should draw some information from previous postgraduate conferences. Learn as much as possible about other linguistic conferences, seminars and workshops, so as to be acquainted with many hints and procedures.

Scene Two — Recreation Services

With the increasing health awareness, more and more travelers have a demand for fitness and spa services in hotel, So an upscale hotel provides wide-ranging facilities, such as a bowling alley, shuffle board, billiards room, fitness room, cards room, KTV, basketball court, tennis court, indoor swimming pool, sauna, beauty salon and others. The recreation center is the place to relax both mind and body. For the hotel, the recreation center is an important vehicle to promote and enhance the hotel's reputation as well as to augment the hotel income.

In this unit, you will learn:

Fitness Center

Beauty Salon

Part 4　Other Services　其他服务英语 | 105

Massage Center

Activities

Fitness Center

Listen to a conversation and complete it by filling in the missing words and expressions as you listen to the dialogue.

Scene: A guest goes to take exercise in the hotel gym.

(R=Receptionist, G=Guest)

R: Good afternoon, sir. Welcome to our _____.

G: Good afternoon. What kinds of exercise can I do here?

R: Various things, like _____, and things like that. We have the latest fitness apparatus here, such as racing apparatus, _____, spring expanders, dumb-bells and so on. You name it.

G: Sounds great! What Exercise can I do to develop my _____?

R: You may use dumbbells. Let me show you. Sit down here and hold one dumbbell in _____. Then, use your thighs to get yourself in position. Raise the dumbbells up to _____ while ensuring that your palms are _____. Push the dumbbells upwards and lift them up until they are fully _____ _____. Lower back the dumbbells down to your ear level. Then repeat this.

G: Cool. I'll have a try.

R: I think you'd better _____ in order to avoid muscle injury.

G: Oh, I see. Thanks for your reminding me.

R: What else can I do for you?

G: Could you _____ for me?

R: Sure, I'll be back soon. Enjoy.

Useful Expressions

What kinds of exercise can I do here?

Various things, like **jogging, stretching, weight-lifting,** and things like that.

We have the latest fitness apparatus here, such as racing apparatus, exercise bicycle, spring expanders, dumb-bells and so on. **You name it.**

What Exercise can I do to **develop my shoulder muscles**?

Then, use your thighs to **get yourself in position**.

Raise the dumbbells up to ear level while ensuring that your palms are facing forward.

Push the dumbbells upwards and lift them up until they are fully extended on top of your head.

I think you'd better warm up first **in order to avoid muscle injury**.

Practice:

Introduce one of the following exercise in English in class.

Yoga	Aerobics	Spinning	Treadmill
Free-weight dumbbell	Chest press machine		

Beauty Salon

Listen to the dialogue and answer the following questions:

a. How does the guest let the staff know the hair style she likes?

b. Does the guest decide how long her hair will be?

c. What's the guest's worry about having highlights?

d. Are the highlights to be pronounced or subtle?

e. Is the guest satisfied with her new hair style?

Useful Expressions

Have you taken a look at **any of the new styles lately**?

Do you want to **keep your hair long**? Or do you want to **make it shorter**?

Perhaps you should **go even shorter** than in the picture.

I'll **leave it up to you**.

You should really think about getting highlights put in, too.

We can **do a little bit** this time. If you like it, we can **do more** next time.

Otherwise, **the highlights should grow out** in about four weeks.

What do you think of it?

Practice:

Here are some phrases about hairdressing below. Choose the right phrases corresponding to the Chinese.

permanent,	scissors	hair dryer	hair cutting
gel	dandruff	hair coloring	thinning
blow	hair designer	have a shampoo	hair treatment
comb	hairspray	hairdresser	hair clip

洗头（　　）	烫发（　　）	剪发（　　）
打薄（　　）	护发（　　）	染发（　　）
吹风（　　）	吹风机（　　）	梳子（　　）
发夹（　　）	剪刀（　　）	发胶（　　）
定型液（　　）	头皮屑（　　）	发型造型师（　　）
美发从业人员（　　）		

Massage Center

Listen to the dialogue about sauna and massage service and finish the information in the form below.

Guest's Name:
Room Number:
Massage Types in Hotel:
Guest's Choice:
Massage Is Helpful for:
When the point is pressed, you might feel:
Charge for The Massage:

Useful Expressions

Welcome to our **spa center**, sir!
We have **body massage, foot massage and point massage.** Which one would you like?
Point massage is **a typical Chinese massage**.
When one point is massaged, **the corresponding organ will feel better** if it is hurt.
Besides, **Massage is helpful to** relax muscles, relieve stress and improve the circulation.
But when the point is pressed, **you might feel a bit sore**.
You can tell the masseuse **if she is pressing too hard**.

Practice:

Mr. Brown is on the phone, consulting the massage service in the hotel. He plans to make a reservation for himself and his wife this evening. The receptionist introduces different kinds of massage treatment, the cost, the methods of payment and the service hours in details. Make a dialogue with your partner.

Vocabulary

apparatus	[ˌæpəˈreɪtəs]	n.	仪器，器械
circulation	[sɜːkjəˈleɪʃn]	n.	流通，血液循环
corresponding	[ˌkɒrəˈspɒndɪŋ]	adj.	相应的，相关的
dumb-bell	[dʌm bel]	n.	哑铃
extend	[ɪkˈstend]	v.	延伸，扩展
fantastic	[fænˈtæstɪk]	adj.	极好的
gym	[dʒɪm]	n.	健身房
hairdo	[ˈheəduː]	n.	发型，做头发
highlight	[ˈhaɪlaɪt]	n.	高光，挑染
jog	[dʒɒg]	v.	慢跑
massage	[ˈmæsɑːʒ]	n. / v.	按摩
muscle	[ˈmʌsl]	n.	肌肉
organ	[ˈɔːgən]	n.	器官，机构
palm	[pɑːm]	n.	手掌，手心
recreation	[ˌrekriˈeɪʃn]	n.	娱乐，消遣
relieve	[rɪˈliːv]	v.	缓解，减除
sore	[sɔː(r)]	adj.	疼痛的
stretch	[stretʃ]	v.	伸展
stress	[stres]	n.	压力，强调
subtle	[ˈsʌtl]	adj.	不明显的，微妙的
sure	[ʃʊə(r)]	v.	确保
fitness center			健身中心
race apparatus			跑步机
spring expander			弹簧扩展器
warm up			热身
weight-lift			举重

Exercises

I. Please translate the following sentences:
1. 您想剪什么发式？
2. 您能给我看一些发型的式样吗？

Part 4　Other Services　其他服务英语 | 109

3. 我想做运动。能不能告诉我这里有什么运动设施?
4. 在健身前您最好做伸展运动。
5. 按摩有助于放松肌肉，缓解压力和促进血液循环。
6. I think you would look cute with short hair.
7. Please relax with your eyes closed and breathe calmly.
8. This exercise will help build your shoulders.
9. Can you show me how to use this machine?
10. Would you like to have a shampoo?

II Match the terms in column A with the meanings in column B.

Column A	Column B
A. bathing service	a. 保健服务
B. health care service	b. 保龄球馆
C. entertainment service	c. 会员费
D. physician scales	d. 室内游泳池
E. bowling room	e. 香草泡浴
F. medical examinations	f. 娱乐服务
G. recreational facilities	g. 洗浴服务
H. membership fee	h. 体检
I. indoor pool	i. 体重秤
J. fragrant herbal bath	j. 康乐设施

III Look at the following pictures and describe each one with at least five sentences.

Tips

How to Exercise Safely?

One key to exercising safely is the warm-up phase. For six to ten minutes, do a low-intensity version of the activity, to loosen up muscles and make you less prone to injury. A good technique also protects you. Activity by activity, here are some of the most common aerobic pitfalls and how to avoid them.

Cycling

When cycling, pay special attention to your seat height. Position the seat so that when you extend one leg fully on the down pedal, with your foot flat, that knee is slightly bent. If the seat is too low, you will stress your knees. If it is too high, you will put undue force on your lower back. But when the seat is properly positioned, you will work the intended muscles——the quads (on the fronts of the thighs) and the gluteus (in the buttocks).

Walking

When you walk, jog or run, strike the ground with your heel first, then with the ball of your foot, and finally push off from your toes. This heel-ball-toe pattern helps to prevent shin splints and shin pain. For activities that involve jumping, such as rope jumping or step aerobics, the pattern is reversed: toe-ball-heel. Sport-specific footwear is designed to absorb impact at those parts of the foot that strike the ground most directly. For example, aerobic dance shoes are most padded at the ball of the foot, while running shoes have more cushioning at the heel.

Using a Rowing Machine

If you are exercising on a rowing machine, maintain proper posture by always keeping your shoulders aligned directly over your hips. Avoid the common mistake of sliding your seat backward before you move your arms. Instead, slide back and pull at the same time. If you don't follow this technique you risk straining your lower back. To protect your joints, try never to lock your knees or elbows.

Using a Stair Climber Exercise Machine

If you are using a stair climber, avoid over stressing your knees by keeping your extended leg slightly bent and both knees aligned behind your toes; if necessary, lean back a bit. Also, avoid the common mistake of resting your forearms along the handrails for support. People have developed elbow tendinitis and carpal tunnel syndrome from overextending their elbows and wrists while on a stair climber.

Swimming

Take a few swimming lessons if you have not done so recently. New techniques help to prevent shoulder problems and allow you to swim more efficiently. The S-patterned stroke gives you more thrust because your arms push against still water, not their own choppy wake. As shown below, keep your head down except to breathe; turn it just until your mouth is out of the water. Keep your shoulders higher than your legs, and kick from your hips, not your knees. Try not to arch your back.

Scene Three — Shopping Arcade

For tourists, souvenirs and gifts are not only something they can take home for families and friends, but also revive happy memories of their enjoyable experiences. This creates great opportunities for hotel shops. The hotel shops provide consumer goods, ranging from jewelry, handicrafts, antiques, Chinese paintings and calligraphy to garments, foods, Chinese knots, Chinese cutting, to name just a few. These shops make service the very essence of the gracious tradition of Chinese hospitality. Shopping arcade add much to the convenience and pleasure of guests as well as to the financial success of the hotel.

Part 4   Other Services   其他服务英语 | 111

In this unit, you will learn:

Choosing a Gift

Chinese Porcelain

Chinese Painting

Activities

Choosing a Gift

Listen to the dialogue and mark the following sentences with T (true) or F (false).

1. _____ The guest wants to buy any gift as a token for her China trip.
2. _____ It takes a long time to make a seal with a name.
3. _____ The assistant believes a Qipao is suitable for the customer who has a slim shape.
4. _____ The Qipao is made of cotton.
5. _____ The customer doesn't like the design but the color is her favorite.
6. _____ The customer wants to try on the Qipao.

Useful Expressions

We have **the best souvenirs** in the city.

You could buy **a seal with his name on it.**

What do you think will be the most suitable for me?

Your shape is so **gracious and slim.**

Would you like to have a Chinese Qipao? **It's very popular** in China.

It is made of pure Chinese silk. It's velvety and the **color is brilliant**.
What size are you?

Practice:

Practice the following expressions about bargaining in class.
- Could you give me a discount?
- Can you sell it for four hundred yuan?
- I think that is too dear, Can you come down a bit?
- Could you lower the price some?
- I may give you a 20% discount at most.
- I'm sorry, but the price is final.
- They are sold at a fair price.
- That's our rock bottom price.
- It cannot be further lowered.
- One hundred and fifty yuan , you can't be wrong on that .
- OK, Let's call it a deal.

Chinese Porcelain

Listen to the conversation and complete it by filling in the missing words and expressions as you listen to the dialogue.
Scene: A customer is choosing some porcelain in the shop.

(A= Assistant, C=Customer)

R: What can I do for you?

C: May I have a look at that _____?

R: Yes, of course.

C: It is extremely beautiful. _____?

R: It was made in Jingdezhen, the capital of porcelain.

C: It's very nice, I'll take it.

R: OK. Is there anything else you want, madam?

C: (Pointing to a set of blue and white porcelain tableware) _____ _____ looks nice. May I have a look?

R: Of course. You've made a good choice, madam. This is called egg-shell china. It is known to be "as white as jade and _____". It is not for use, _____.

C: Oh, I see. I heard it is the best quality porcelain and it is also made in Jingdezhen, isn't it?

R: Yes, you're right.

C: Oh, it must be precious. I'll take it.

R: OK. Shall I _____?

C: Separately, please. How much does this all cost?

R: That comes to _____.

C: OK, here's my _____.

Useful Expressions

May I have a look at that china set?

It is extremely beautiful. **Where was it made?**

It was made in Jingdezhen, **the capital city of porcelain.**

It's very nice, **I'll take it.**

The **porcelain tableware** looks nice.

You've made a good choice, madam.

It is known to be "as white as jade and as thin as paper".

It is **not for use, but for show**.

Shall I **wrap them together or separately**?

How much does this **all cost**?

Practice:

Read the following passage. Fill in each blank with appropriate word.

| contribution | recognized | rough | experience | coated |
| primitive | hometown | from | conditions | low |

China is the ①_____ of porcelain and the invention of porcelain was China's great ②_____ to the world civilization. The word china when capitalized is ③_____ as the name of the country. Around 16th century BC in the middle of the Shang Dynasty (17th-11th century BC), the early-stage porcelain appeared in China. The firing techniques were ④_____ in both the bodies and the glazes and the firing temperature was comparatively ⑤_____, so porcelain of that time was called ⑥_____ porcelain for its primitive and transitional nature.

Porcelain derived ⑦_____ pottery. The ancient Chinese ancestors invented porcelain, drawing on the ⑧_____ of firing the white pottery and the hard stamped pottery. Firing porcelain requires the following three ⑨_____ : first, porcelain materials must be porcelain stone, porcelain clay or kaolin, containing rich sericite elements; second, the temperature of kiln stove must be up to 1200℃; third, surface of the vessels must be ⑩_____ with glaze fired in high temperature.

Chinese Painting

Listen to the dialogue and answer the following questions:

a. What's the difference between Western oil paintings and Chinese ink paintings?

b. What kinds of traditional Chinese paintings are there in the shop?

c. What is the cultural indicator of the Chinese national spirit mentioned in the dialogue?

d. What does Chinese art stress?
e. What's the final price of the painting?

Useful Expressions

Could you tell me **the difference between** Western oil paintings **and** Chinese ink paintings?

Oil paintings are created **by colors and brush touches** while traditional Chinese paintings are **by lines and strokes**.

Could you recommend some **traditional Chinese paintings** for me?

We have landscape paintings, figure paintings and flower-and-bird paintings.

Chinese landscape painting is a cultural indicator **of the Chinese national spirit**.

I can almost sense peace and harmony from the painting.

Chinese art stresses **the harmony between Man and Nature**, which is an important part of China's traditional culture.

Can you **come down a bit**?

That's our **rock bottom price**. It cannot be lowered further.

Practice:

A customer wants to buy a Chinese painting for his mother. The shop assistant suggests a painting with cranes for it's a symbol of longevity in China. Make a dialogue with your partner.

Vocabulary

china	['tʃaɪnə]	n.	瓷器，陶具
gracious	['greɪʃəs]	adj.	雅致的
harmony	['hɑ:məni]	n.	和谐，协调
jade	[dʒeɪd]	n.	玉，翡翠
line	[laɪn]	n.	线条
lower	['ləʊə(r)]	v.	降低，减少
porcelain	['pɔ:səlɪn]	n.	瓷，瓷器
seal	[si:l]	n.	印章
shape	[ʃeɪp]	n.	身材，体型
slim	[slɪm]	adj.	苗条的，纤细的
souvenir	[ˌsu:və'nɪə]	n.	纪念品
spirit	['spɪrɪt]	n.	精神，精髓
stress	[stres]	v.	强调
stroke	[strəʊk]	n.	笔画
tableware	['teɪblweə]	n.	餐具

token	[ˈtəʊkən]	n.	象征，代币
velvety	[ˈvelvəti]	adj.	柔软的，光滑的
wrap	[ræp]	v.	包装

cultural indicator	文化标志
figure painting	人物画
flower-and-bird painting	花鸟画
landscape painting	山水画
ink painting	水墨画
oil painting	油画
rock bottom price	最低价

Exercises

I. Please translate the following sentences:
1. 我想为我的亲戚和朋友买一些真正的中国纪念品。
2. 您可以到处看看，看看有没有您喜欢的东西。
3. 从那些山水画中我能找到平静与和谐的感觉。
4. 我们有各种各样的中国古董。
5. 您需要我一起包装还是分开包装？
6. In traditional Chinese thinking, cranes and pine trees symbolize longevity.
7. How much does this jade bracelet cost? It looks nice .
8. All our products are clearly priced.
9. We have good varieties of gifts for you to choose from.
10. Chinese porcelain wares are not only daily handy necessities, but also precious arts and crafts.

II. Discuss the following topics:
1. As a shop assistant, how do you recommend souvenirs to the customers?
2. Suppose you are a shop assistant, what could you say if the guest asks you to give him some discount?
3. Please say some names of the Chinese souvenirs in English.

III. Role-play: Make up a dialogue according to the situation below.

A foreign customer wants to buy some silk scarves for her friends. The shop assistant makes a detailed introduction of the silk scarves, including the types, how to tie and how to wash them. The customer is pleased to take five scarves.

How to Sell a Product?

  The key to most successful businesses or professions is to sell products. When there is a product to sell, there are several things that should be done before marketing begins to ensure that the time and money spent on marketing and advertising is not wasted.

- Assess the product's most unique features. Get to understand the competition's products and what makes yours different from theirs.
- Assess your intended audience or customer base. Find out their basic demographics and what people of that age group or socioeconomic status are looking for in a product like yours. Knowing this will help you sell your product.
- Cast the widest net possible. If your demographic group is narrow, find ways to widen it to make the product appeal to more types of people.
- Get the best advertising possible. Hire professionals to get persuasive advertising copy or visual advertisements. Place the ads everywhere your intended demographic will see them.
- Always give your customers what you have promised. Make sure your claims are persuasive, but honest and achievable.
- Offer excellent customer service in order to stay in business. Treat your customers fairly in order to keep them coming back to buy more. Offer incentives to encourage repeat buys. Stay in communication with customers and clients. Make sure they know where to turn if they have a problem with the product or with your service.
- Keep at it. Keep selling and marketing your product, even if it has not yet made a profit. Remember that many of the most popular and interesting products, services and websites were operated for years before achieving a profit.

Emergencies & Complaints
应急和投诉处理

Part 5

Brainstorm

Please look at the picture of a possible complaint in this hotel, and describe what complaints may happen in the hotel and how to solve it. As a class, list words you used to describe the possible situations and solutions in this hotel. Then discuss them with your groups. See which group has the largest vocabulary.

Complaint about, solution…

Scene One: Handling Emergencies

Break-ins, burglary, fires, natural disasters and terrorist attacks are just a few of the potential threats to travelers' safety in hotel rooms. So safety and security are important factors in guests' selection of a hotel. The hotel sets in-house safety and security systems, such as "well-equipped fire prevention systems in accordance with local regulations", "an emergency plan", "an emergency lighting system", "a 24-h uniformed security guard" and "the regular testing of hotel safety and security systems" to keep the guests safe and satisfied.

In this unit, you will learn:

Asking for a Doctor

Elevator Emergency

Fire Emergency

Part 5 Emergencies & Complaints 应急和投诉处理 | 119

Activities

Asking For a Doctor

Listen to the conversations and complete them by filling in the missing words and expressions as you listen to the dialogues.

Dialogue A:

Scene: A guest gets hurt in the room. Her husband is calling the front desk for help.

(R=Receptionist, G=Guest)

R: Hello, operator speaking May I help you?

G: Hello, this is Mr. Brown _____. There's been _____ in my room.

R: Oh, dear. What's up?

G: My wife has _____ and sprained her ankle. She can't stand up now.

R: I'm sorry to hear that. Please _____. I'll send up _____ to help you.

G: Please be quick. Her ankle hurts badly. I think it might be broken.

R: Don't worry. Our first aid worker is on her way now. I will _____ _____ too.

G: Thanks.

Dialogue B:

Scene: A guest asks the room attendant to get him some medicine.

(A=Attendant, G=Guest)

A: May I come in? It's the room attendant.

G: Come in please. I'm not feeling good. I've got _____ and have loose bowels.

A: I'm sorry to hear that. You really look so pale. Would you like me to _____ _____ for you?

G: Not necessary. But could you _____ for me?

A: Certainly, sir. I'll do it immediately.

G: Could you please _____?

A: Here you are.

Useful Expressions

What's up?

My wife has **slipped in the bathroom and sprained her ankle**.

I'm sorry to hear that.

Please **remain still**. I'll **send up a fist aid worker** to help you.

Our first aid worker is **on her way** now. I will **call an ambulance** too.

I've got a terrible stomach ache and **have** loose bowels.

You really **look so pale**. Would you like me to **call a doctor** for you?

But could you **get some medicine** for me?

Practice:

Mr. Hepworth has a stomachache in his room now. He makes a phone call to ask the hotel staff to bring him some medicine. Make a dialogue with your classmate.

Elevator Emergency

Listen to the dialogue and answer the following questions:

a. On which floor does the lift stop?

b. How many people are there stuck in the lift?

c. What should the guests do in the lift?

d. What should the guests avoid doing in the lift?

e. How long did the technicians take to get the guests out?

Useful Expressions

I'm **stuck in the lift**.

Calm down, madam. The technicians are **on their way**.

Is there **anyone else** with you?

Please **do not** force the lift door open with your hands, **not try to** climb out from the lift.

Relax and **we'll get you out soon**.

I pressed the **emergency button**! And then I **stayed in the elevator** waiting to be rescued.

Practice:

Describe the following picture.

Fire Emergency

Listen to five announcements and fill in the missing words and expressions.

1. "Ladies and gentlemen, attention please. _____ in the building and we are investigating the situation. _____ and listen to the speaker for _____. Thank you!"

2. "Ladies and gentlemen, attention please. We _____ and found it to be a false alarm. We regret any inconvenience caused. Thank you."

3. "Ladies and gentlemen, attention please. There is _____ in the building. Please evacuate by the nearest exit staircase and _____ given by the fire wardens. Do remember to _____."

4. Ladies and gentleman, attention please! There is a small fire in hotel but it is already _____, so please remain calm. For your safety, please follow me to the lobby _____.Please leave your luggage behind and don't use the elevator. _____.

5. "Ladies and gentlemen, attention please. The emergency situation in the building is now under control. We _____. Thank you."

Useful Expressions

Ladies and gentlemen, **attention please**.
Please **do not panic** and listen to the speaker for **further instruction**.
We regret **any inconvenience** caused.
There exists **an emergency situation** in the building.
Please **evacuate** by the nearest exit staircase and **obey** all instructions given by the fire wardens.
Do remember to avoid the use of lifts.
There is a small fire in hotel but it is already **under control**.
For your safety, please follow me to the lobby using the **emergency exit**.
Thank you for your **cooperation**.

Practice:

Discuss the following question: "What are the common fire hazards in the hotel?"

Vocabulary

alarm	[əˈlɑːm]	n.	警报，闹铃
ambulance	[ˈæmbjələns]	n.	救护车
ankle	[ˈæŋkl]	n.	踝关节，脚踝
bowel	[ˈbaʊəl]	n.	肠

cooperation	[kəʊˌɒpəˈreɪʃn]	n.	合作
exit	[ˈeksɪt]	n.	出口，通道
evacuate	[ɪˈvækjueɪt]	v.	撤离，疏散
inconvenience	[ˌɪnkənˈviːniəns]	n.	不便，麻烦
instruction	[ɪnˈstrʌkʃn]	n.	指令，指导
investigate	[ɪnˈvestɪgeɪt]	v.	调查
panic	[ˈpænɪk]	v.	惊恐
regret	[rɪˈgret]	v.	后悔，遗憾
slip	[slɪp]	v.	滑，滑倒
sprain	[spreɪn]	v.	扭伤
staircase	[ˈsteəkeɪs]	n.	楼梯
technician	[tekˈnɪʃn]	n.	技术人员
warden	[ˈwɔːdn]	n.	看守人，管理员
first aid worker			急救人员
fire alarm			火警
fire emergency			火灾
fire warden			防火指挥员

Exercises

I. Please translate the following sentences:

1. 我先生晕倒了。
2. 我牙疼得厉害，能帮我买些药吗？
3. 需要我为您叫医生吗？
4. 我们最好先按警铃，然后待在电梯里等待救助。
5. 不要着急，这只是消防演习。
6. Let me put some iodine on the cut.
7. Please relax. A doctor is on the way.
8. I was stuck between 10th and 11th floors in the elevator.
9. In case of an emergency, follow the instructions written inside the elevator and try to keep others calm.
10. Please obey all instructions given by the fire wardens and evacuate by the nearest exit staircase.

II. Discuss the following topics:

1. You are part of the front desk staff when you receive a call from hotel personnel that there is a fire. What do you do?
2. You are delivering room service when you smell smoke from a room at the end

Part 5   Emergencies & Complaints   应急和投诉处理 | 123

of the hall. Then the alarm goes off. What should you do?

III. Please match the words with the pictures and describe the response to each emergency.

typhoon — ( )	fire — ( )	heart attack — ( )
loss of property — ( )	elevator accident — ( )	power failure — ( )
tumble — ( )		

a. _____   b. _____   c. _____

d. _____   e. _____   f. _____

g. _____

Tips

How to Escape a Stranded Elevator?

There are few situations worse than being trapped in an elevator to elevate the pulse of anyone afraid of heights, confined spaces, or both. If you should ever find yourself lodged unfortunately between floors. Here is just about everything you should do to ensure a speedy escape.

Step 1

Stay Calm. As soon as you realize you're stranded, you may feel a natural urge to panic. However, you have to tell yourself to put mind over matter, and to stay as calm as possible. If you start panicking, your body will start to feel the effects, and you'll only be making it more difficult for yourself to think clearly, and therefore making it harder for you to find a way to escape.

Step 2

Find a light source if the lights are out. If the elevator is dark, you can create some light by using a key chain flash light or opening your cell phone or PDA. Try your best not to keep the device on for so long that battery power is drained. Creating light will help you see the buttons and get a better sense of your situation.

Step 3

Press the call button. If it's dark, use the light source to find the call button. Then, press the call button to contact a technician to help you. This will alert maintenance personnel there is a problem with the elevator.

Step 4

If there's no answer, try calling for help. If there is no response to pressing the call button, check your cell phone for reception. If you have any reception, call your local emergency services number. If there is still no response, press the alarm button a few times.

Step 5

Press the "door open" button. Sometimes, this button can just get jammed, and if you press it, it'll open the elevator right up.

• You can also try the "door close" button, which may have gotten jammed as well.

• You can also try pressing the button of a floor below where the elevator is currently resting.

Step 6

If you can't call for help, try to get the attention of the people outside the elevator. You can try to bang on the door of the elevator with shoes or other objects and yell to alert passersby. Depending on the sound transmittance of the door, tapping firmly with a key on the door may make a loud sound throughout the elevator shaft.

Step 7

Wait it out. If you are not in an extreme life-or-death situation, just wait it out. In a best case scenario, people will notice the elevator is not working in minutes and you'll be out in no time. People frequently use the elevator and people in the building, especially building personnel, should quickly notice that something is off.

Scene Two — Settling Complaints

Hotels should never forget that the best way to advertise their service is through a satisfied customer. If a customer is dissatisfied, he will give negative feedback and bad reviews about the hotel and its services. The key to running a successful hotel is customer service. A major aspect of this is directly addressing customer's complaints and ensuring that these complaints are resolved to the customer's satisfaction.

Part 5 Emergencies & Complaints 应急和投诉处理 | 125

Successful resolution will have a positive effect on the customer, who will be more open to returning to the hotel in the future, as the way the complaint was handled and resolved makes the customer feel special and shows him that the hotel is genuinely interested in keeping its customers happy and satisfied.

In this unit, you will learn:

Settling Complaints about Reservation

Settling Complaints about Room Facilities

Settling Complaints about Food

Activities

Settling Complaints About Reservation

Listen to a conversation and complete it by filling in the missing words and expressions as you listen to the dialogue.

Scene: A guest comes to the hotel to check in, when the receptionist finds the room reserved by the guest has been let to another guest.

(R=Receptionist, C=Customer)

R: Good evening. Welcome to our hotel. What can I do for you?

G: Yes, I have a reservation with you.

R: _____?

G: John Smith.

R: Just a moment, please. I'll _____ ... Sorry, I'm afraid we have no record of your reservation. When and where was it made?

G: It was made online _____ from Beijing.

R: Wait a moment, please. I'll check our reservation again ... Thank you for waiting, sir. I'm sorry, but the room has been _____.

G: What! How could you do that to me?

R: Calm down. Look, it's 9 p.m. now. We thought you would not come tonight, because we only hold the room reservation till 6 p.m. It is _____.

G: You should have _____ before you let the room to others! Can't you give me another single room?

R: We're awfully sorry. But I'm afraid no single room is available.

G: I reserved the room in advance, but you still have no room for me! I'd never _____ _____.

R: We do apologize for the inconvenience. Maybe we can offer you _____ _____ with the same room rate of a single room.

G: If that's the case ... alright.

R: Thank you for _____.

Useful Expressions

In whose name was the reservation made?/ Who made the reservation?

I'll check **the reservation record**.

Sorry, I'm afraid we **have no record of** your reservation.

I'm sorry, but the room has been **let to somebody else**.

We thought you would not come tonight, because we only **hold the room reservation till 6 p.m.** It is the **hotel policy**.

I'd never expected **such a thing to happen**.

We do apologize for the inconvenience.

Maybe we can offer you a standard room **with the same room rate** of a single room.

Practice:

Say some sentences about how to express apology to the guest.

Settling Complaints About Room Facilities

Listen to the dialogue and answer the following questions:

a. Which room is the call from?

b. Why is the guest unhappy with her room?

c. What have the hotel been busy with?

d. Who will be sent to repair the television?

e. What will the guest do while waiting for the room?

Useful Expressions

I've just checked in and **I'm not happy with** my room.
May I know what is wrong?
I didn't expect these things would happen in your hotel!
I'm terribly sorry to hear that.
We have been extremely busy **with a large conference**.
What's more, **it's the peak season**. We might have **overlooked** some points.
I'm sorry for your inconvenience, but **I'm afraid** there is no vacant room now.
I promise everything **will be in order soon**.
Would you like to have a drink in our lobby with our compliments?

Practice:

Discuss how to deal with a complaint.

Settling Complaints About Food

Listen to the dialogue and answer the following questions:

a. Why has the service been so slow?
b. How would the guest like his steak to be done?
c. What does the waitress do after the guest complains about the steak?
d. Why does the guest complain again?
e. What does the waitress do to express regret for the trouble?

Useful Expressions

The service has been **really slow**!
As you can see, it has been a very busy evening.
Several large groups came in **at the same time as you**, and I agree some guests have to wait.
The steak is **over-cooked and tough. What I want** is a medium steak.
I'll send it **back to the kitchen** and get another one for you.
We're **extremely sorry** about it, sir.
I really must **apologize for** the situation. I'll get it right away.
To express our regret for the trouble, we can offer you two complimentary desserts and **a 30% discount** from the meal.

Practice:

The guest goes to have buffet in a hotel. She finds the tableware is not clean after being seated. Then the seafood and coffee have run out, and not been refilled. The guest is very unsatisfied. The restaurant supervisor explains and apologies to the guest. Make a dialogue in class.

Vocabulary

cappuccino	[ˌkæpuˈtʃiːnəʊ]	n.	卡布奇诺
complaint	[kəmˈpleɪnt]	n.	抱怨，投诉
confirmation	[ˌkɒnfəˈmeɪʃn]	n.	确认
housemaid	[ˈhaʊsmeɪd]	n.	客房服务员，女仆
inconvenience	[ˌɪnkənˈviːniəns]	n.	不方便，麻烦
overlook	[ˌəʊvəˈlʊk]	v.	忽视，远眺
stain	[steɪn]	n.	污点，瑕疵
tough	[tʌf]	adj.	坚硬的
get one's point			理解
over-cooked			烹饪过久的
peak season			旺季
reservation record			预订记录
to express our regret			为表歉意

Exercises

I. Please translate the following sentences:
1. 我马上派一位客房服务员上来。
2. 我马上去查清这件事情。
3. 我的菜还没上来。怎么要这么久的时间呢?
4. 如果您把行李整理好，我们就安排您到别的房间去。
5. 我们为给您带来不便深表歉意。
6. The toilet is clogged. When I flushed it, it overflowed.
7. The previous guest checked out very late while you demanded immediate access to your room. So the chambermaid didn't have time to make up the room.
8. To express our regret for all the trouble, we offer you a 10% discount off/ a complimentary flowers basket.
9. You put the "DND" sign on the knob, so the chambermaid didn't make up the room.
10. I'm terribly sorry. I'll send an engineer straight up.

II. Role-play:

Mr. Jenny Brown in room 1023 calls the receptionist Cindy at the Front Desk because the water closet (抽水马桶) can't be used, and there is no hot water.He shows his dissatisfaction.

Cindy apologizes to Mr. Jenny Brown. She explains the water pipe is being repaired, and she will send a repairman to repair the water closet within five minutes.

III. Writing

Suppose you are the General Manager of Crown Plaza Hotel, write a reply to the letter of complaint sent by Jane Clinton who was disappointed to receive poor service during her stay with your hotel.

Crown Plaza Hotel
No.17, 4th Block, 1st Ring Road,
Hangzhou, Zhejiang

Attn: Mr. Lin Yunzhi
Dear Mr. Lin,

As one of your regular guests, I'm writing to complain about my stay in your hotel.
To be frank, I am terribly disappointed at your service as well as your hotel facilities. Firstly, when I checked in, your receptionists chatted aloud. I had waited for almost twenty minutes before my luggage was sent to my room. Moreover, the tap was out of order when I took a shower. Worst of all, the hotel failed to provide us with room service next morning. I find it unacceptable that you sold us a room, that was not similar to the description on your website, and therefore I claim a refund of RMB800.
I sincerely hope that you could look into this matter and the problems mentioned above can be solved at your earliest convenience.

Yours sincerely
Jane Clinton

Outline:

1. Your apologies and sympathies
2. Measures you will take
3. Compensation you will make
4. Your wish to offer better service

Tips

How to Deal with Customer's Complaints?

1. Listening is the key. First listen to the customer and figure out what his problem is.

2. Be sure not to show feelings towards the situation; let the customer tell everything that has gone wrong in the situation.

3. To show him you are listening. Nod or say something to him to let him know, this may make it a little more comfortable for the customer to just relax.

4. Show how sincere. Showing that you understand the customer and want to be able to help him with his problem is now in your mind. Now that he has told everything it may be safer to show a little feeling toward the whole thing. Maybe show how sorry the store is for his inconvenience. Doing this will not only make the situation a little better, but will make the customer see someone cares about his problem.

5. Figure out the situation. Now that the customer has said everything and has realized you want to fix his problem and act on it: Now try to figure out what really has upset the customer and find an answer to it.

6. Nothing looks worse than showing there is no idea what to do, even if the situation is hard, looking like there is some idea of what to do. Facial expression is the key, try to smile with the customer at all times, do not show confusion.

7. Answer to the problem. Figuring out what to do about the complaint is the hardest part, there are probably solutions to helping the customer, but one will stick out as the best answer to the complaint that will work, act on it and aim to make the customer happy as soon as possible. The longer he has to wait the more frustrated he will get.

8. If at any point realization of being unable to answer the customer's complaint comes to mind, find someone else that may be able to. Do this as soon as possible, to avoid confusion between both you and the customer.

9. The best person to help out. A manager, or an associate that has been through a similar situation that is going on. If you can not find someone to help you with the situation, tell the customer politely that while wanting to help them, you don't want to point them in the wrong direction and tell them something that may not be correct.

10. After getting the situation under control and hopefully fixed. Apologize for the inconvenience to the customer and hope it doesn't affect his impression on the company. Maybe throwing in a nice, "Have a nice day" could throw a smile onto the customer's face.

11. Improve service or product quality to avoid similar problem from happening again.

Hotel Management & Orientation
酒店管理与求职

Part 6

Brainstorm

Please look at the picture of the hotel, and describe the jobs of hotel management. As a class, list words you used to describe the possible staff and places in this hotel. Then discuss them with your groups. See which group has the largest vocabulary.

people, places ...

English For Hotel Staff
Developing Skills

酒店实用英语（灵活应用篇）

Scene One — Hotel Management

Businesses require competent management to get work completed in a timely manner. The hotel business requires especially resourceful managers due to the fast-paced environment. Managing a hotel, even a small one, is a sizable task. Managers handle everything from organizing the hotel staff to dealing with customer's complaints. Effective management of a hotel is not easy, but it can be rewarding. The functions of management are planning, organizing, staffing, leading and controlling. The management is the decisive factor which makes or ruins a hotel.

In this unit, you will learn:

Promotion

Interviews & Orientation

Activities

Promotion

Listen to the dialogue and answer the following questions:

a. Who is making a group reservation with the sales manager?
b. What does the sales manager give to Mr. Cooper to show the different room rates?
c. Were the room rates the same in the peak season, the mid season and the low season?
d. Is the price for a group negotiable?
e. How can payment be made for a group reservation?

Useful Expressions

I want **to take up some of your time to** discuss the reservations for our groups.

I'm glad to hear that and **we feel honored that you have chosen our hotel**.

Here's **a copy of our tariff**. We have different rates for groups and for FIT and for different periods of the year, that is, **the peak season, the mid season and the low season**.

May I ask if you **give preferential rates to groups**?

We usually offer **40% discount off** for large groups like yours.

Can you give us **a bigger discount** for such a big group?

I'm not in a position to agree to such a big reduction.

We will **bill you based on your credit limit** and you do not have to pay in advance.

If you **agree to the terms**, please sign and return a fax copy to us.

Practice:

Please discuss the following question: " What is the underlying goal for F&B Promotion in the hotel?"

Interviews & Orientation

Read the sentences. Listen to the interview in a hotel. And put the applicant's responses in the correct order.

1. _____ I think the most important one is flexibility to respond to a range of different work situations.
2. _____ I definitely plan to stay in the hotel industry, serving guests.
3. _____ Thank you, Ms. Li. And thank you too, Ms. Wei and Mr. Zhu, for your time.
4. _____ Well, what benefits can I get from the position?
5. _____ I like to know the different functions associated with food and beverages, supervising staff and planning various functions inside the restaurant.
6. _____ Besides, I'm positive, organized, good at communication and have 8 years previous Food & Beverage industry experience.
7. _____ Well, I think the position of Assistant Food & Beverage Manager is a bigger challenge to me.

Useful Expressions

What is it that **attracts you to the position**?

Why do you believe you're **a good fit for** Food & Beverage Assistant?

What values do you think you share with us?

Besides, **I'm positive, organized, good at communication** and have 8 years previous Food & Beverage industry experience.

We do value the effort to provide a globally recognized hospitality experience and think **it's a key to our success**.

What are your **long-term objectives**?

Thanks for coming. We'll finish reviewing all the candidates in the next couple of days.

If you're selected for the position, we'll **notify you by email**.

Practice:

Work with a partner. Take turns to interview each other. Ask your partner questions about his or her past, and hopes and plans for the future.

Settling Complaints About Reservation

Listen to the conversation about orientation and complete it by filling in the missing words and expressions as you listen to the dialogue.
Scene: A new employee reports on his first day of work. The Training Manager is talking to him.

(E= employee, M= Manager)

M: Good morning. Welcome to our hotel. It's your first day of work at our hotel, isn't it?

E: Yes.

M: According to our _____, every new employee is required to attend an _____ in the first week.

E: What can I expect to find out?

M: The hotel history and culture, _____ and its properties, the functions of our hotel departments as well as _____.

E: Oh, so much information I need to remember!

M: Don't worry. We'll give you _____ before training which has detailed descriptions in it. You are now _____ so general _____ should be applied during working times.

E: I see. Could you be more specific?

M: OK. You should wear _____ provided by the hotel during working hours. Have a neat and _____ at all times. You should pay attention to your hair, uniform, shoes and nails. Your hair should be above the collar of the shirt. Your uniform must _____. Shoes should be properly polished. Nails must be well trimmed and clean. And you are not allowed to _____.

E: I see.

M: The image of the hotel is reflected by the professionalism of the staff, so you must know our hotel's _____ well. Be courteous and cheerful at all time.

E: OK. What else do I need to know?

M: Well, when you come to work, don't bring your _____ to the work place.

E: Thank you for all your information.

M: You're welcome.

Useful Expressions

According to our hotel's regulations, every new employee is required to attend an orientation meeting on the first day.

We'll give you a handbook before training which has **detailed descriptions** in it.

You are now **a representative of our hotel**, so general grooming and standards should be applied during working times.

You should wear hotel uniforms provided by the hotel **during working hours**.

Have a **neat and professional appearance** at all times.

You are **not allowed** to have a beard.

You **must know** our hotel's specialties and services well.

Be courteous and cheerful **at all time**.

Practice:

Discuss with your partner about how to answer the calls professionally.

Vocabulary

agreement	[əˈgriːmənt]	n.	协议，合同书
candidate	[ˈkændɪdət]	n.	求职者，候选人
cohesiveness	[kəʊˈhiːsɪvnəs]	n.	凝聚
courteous	[ˈkɜːtiəs]	adj.	有礼貌的，殷勤的
grooming	[ˈgruːmɪŋ]	n.	装束，打扮
handbook	[ˈhændbʊk]	n.	手册，指南
honored	[ˈhɒnɔːd]	adj.	光荣的，荣幸的
host	[həʊst]	v.	做东道主，举办宴会
tariff	[ˈtærɪf]	n.	价格表
term	[tɜːm]	n.	条款
objective	[əbˈdʒektɪv]	n.	目标，任务
orientation	[ˌɔːriənˈteɪʃn]	n.	任职培训，方向，定位
oversee	[ˌəʊvəˈsiː]	v.	监督，监管
positive	[ˈpɒzətɪv]	adj.	积极的，肯定的
preferential	[ˌprefəˈrenʃl]	adj.	优先的，优惠的
professionalism	[prəˈfeʃənəlɪzəm]	n.	职业化，职业水准
regulation	[ˌregjuˈleɪʃn]	n.	规则，规章
representative	[ˌreprɪˈzentətɪv]	n.	代表
reputation	[ˌrepjuˈteɪʃn]	n.	名誉，名声
supervise	[ˈsuːpəvaɪz]	v.	监督，管理，指导

trim	[trɪm]	v.	修剪
uniform	['ju:nɪfɔ:m]	n.	制服
uphold	[ʌp'həʊld]	v.	支持，维持
wrap up			圆满完成，圆满结束
Assistant Food & Beverage Manager			餐饮部副经理
annual meeting			年会
low season			淡季
mid season			平季
peak season			旺季

Exercises

I. Please translate the following sentences:

1. 我们将在网上公布出折扣信息。
2. 特价房有"住一送一"的活动。
3. 你为什么离职呢？
4. 你能承受工作上的压力吗？
5. 你应该牢记酒店的规章制度。
6. We have a loyalty card scheme for regular customers.
7. My past work experience is closely related to this job. I am confident of doing the job well. Therefore I am desirous to get this post.
8. How do you rate yourself as a professional?
9. How do you handle your conflict with your colleagues in your work?
10. From now on, you are a representative of the our hotel, personal cleanliness and proper grooming are essential.

II. Role-play: Make a dialogue according to the information below.

Student A: Suppose you are a Human Resource Manager working in Grand Hotel. You are interviewing a candidate and find out if he is qualified for the job or not.

Student B: You want to find a job in Grand Hotel as a receptionist. You have the experience of working at the front desk in another hotel for three years. You can speak Chinese and English. You want to show the manager that you are qualified for the job. Remember to answer the questions clearly and politely.

III. Read the passage through carefully and select one word for each blank from the form below the passage.

Top 5　Job Interview Tips

1. **Do your research**

    Fail to plan, and you plan to fail. You are certain to be ___(1)___ specific questions about the ___(2)___, so make sure you've done your ___(3)___ on things like their last year's profits and latest product launches. Also take a ___(4)___ at the latest developments in the industry so you can converse with confidence.

2. **Practice your answers**

    Although there is no set format ___(5)___ every job interview will follow, there are some questions that you can almost ___(6)___ will crop up. You should prepare answers to some of the most common interview questions about your personal strengths and ___(7)___, as well as being able to explain ___(8)___ you would be the best person for the job.

3. **Look the part**

    Appearances shouldn't matter, but the plain fact is that you are often judged before you've even uttered a word. Make sure your shoes are ___(9)___, your clothes fit correctly and that your accessories are subtle. Dressing one level above the job you're ___(10)___ for shows a desire to succeed.

4. **Stay calm**

    Good ___(11)___ is the key to staying in control. Plan your route, allowing extra time for any unexpected delays and get everything you need to take with you ready the night before. Remember to speak ___(12)___, smile and remember that your interviewers are just ___(13)___ people, and they may be nervous too!

5. **Ask questions**

    You should always have some questions for your interviewer to demonstrate your ___(14)___ in the position. Prepare a minimum of five questions, some which will give you more ___(15)___ about the job and some which delve deeper ___(16)___ the culture and goals of the company.

(A) applying	(B) clearly	(C) asked	(D) look
(E) company	(F) homework	(G) interest	(H) that
(I) into	(J) guarantee	(K) weakness	(L) polished
(M) information	(N) preparation	(O) normal	(P) why

How to Conduct a Job Interview?

No. 1: When you conduct a job interview, you will have several goals in mind:

- You want to be confident that your new hire has the skills to do his job well. While human resources will try to verify the information on his resume, you know your department's needs best. You will have to make sure the person you choose can do what is expected of him.

- When a new person joins a department, its dynamic changes. Since this is inevitable, you want to do everything possible to make sure it is a positive change. A big part of any job interview is learning about the job candidate's personality and temperament in order to make sure he will fit in and work well with everyone else.
- Finally, you need to make sure you "click" with your new employee. You aren't looking for a new friend, but you are seeking someone with whom you will have a good working relationship.

No. 2: What Questions Should You (and Should You Not) Ask?

Here are some general examples of good job interview questions. You should develop a list of more specific ones that are relevant to the content of each person's resume.

- Tell me about yourself.
- What are your strengths and weaknesses?
- What did you like best and least about working for your prior employee?
- Tell me about your past manager. What was it like to work for him or her?
- If we hire you, what do you hope to accomplish here?
- Tell me what you know about our company.
- What would you do if you disagreed with me or a coworker?
- Have you ever had a boss you didn't like? What happened?

You should pay careful attention to the answers you get. This is where good listening skills, and most importantly, excellent interpersonal skills, come in. Realize it isn't always the answers to the questions that are most important. What is often most telling is how the candidate reacts to your questions and what he doesn't say.

No. 3: What Should You Do on the Job Interview?

How you act on the interview is as important as how the interviewee does. First of all, treat job candidates with respect—just as you would like to be treated if the tables were turned. It's very important to be polite and considerate.

Try to establish a good rapport with each individual. It will help you get more honest answers. Again, your interpersonal skills will come in very handy!

Remember to be yourself and be truthful. That means you shouldn't give the candidate a false impression about what you are like, what the company is like or what the job will be like.

Scene Two — Career and Resume

A resume is a key tool in the job hunt; it serves the purpose of interview. A resume is an efficient medium for an recruiter to get an overview of your accomplishments and expertise. Employers are always in search of easy ways to find potential candidates and a resume is a piece of paper which is designed for that purpose. As it has so much significance in your job hunt, it needs to be perfect and effective enough to grab the attention of the recruiter. An effective and impressive resume is one which reflects your education, honors, special skills, additional experience, co-curricular activities, awards that you have achieved and accomplished.

In this unit, you will learn:

Career Advice

Resume Templates

Activities

Career Advice

Listen to a passage about career planning process. Please complete it by filling in the missing words and expressions as you listen to it.

What is the Career Planning Process?

The Career Planning Process includes the stages involved in discovering a career path, including _____, research, decision making, _____, and accepting a job offer.

Step 1: Self-assessment is a vital and often overlooked step in planning your various _____. In order to evaluate the suitability of work options, it is important to know who you are as a person. This involves taking a careful inventory of your current _____, interests, skills and _____.

A career counselor can help you with this process through counseling, Exercise and interest/personality inventories.

Once you have articulated a sense of the _____ you would like to derive from your work and the skills you have to offer employers, you can begin your research. This stage involves brainstorming _____ and investigating them thoroughly. You will learn about the _____ and _____ for positions, typical entry points and advancement, satisfactions, frustrations, and other important facts in order to determine if there is a good fit.

Step 2: Research—Online resources are available to help you with your preliminary information gathering.

The next step will be to speak with as many people as possible that are involved in work that is of interest to you. By _____ these individuals for _____ and _____ about their work, you will be getting an insider's perspective about realities of the field and recommended preparation, including _____.

Internships and _____ jobs are an excellent way to sample a field of interest.

They provide the _____ to perform some of the job functions, _____ others' work and _____ the environment. Some individuals observe professionals in various fields for a shorter period of time than an internship. These job shadowing experiences, or externships, can last from one morning to several weeks.

Step 3: _____ involves an evaluation of the pros and cons for the options you have been researching. It also involves prioritizing and, for some, _____. Since the landscape of the world-of-work is constantly changing, it may be _____ to aim for decisions based on absolute certainty.

Adaptability, the ability to manage several options at once, and the ability to maintain a _____ when faced with uncertainty may be easy for some while others may find these traits a stretch. Self-awareness, occupational awareness and intuition can all _____ your decision-making.

Step 4: Search—Once you have identified a work objective, you can begin your job search. Most people will be involved with activities such as networking, identifying prospective employers, writing _____ and _____, and _____.

Step 5: Acceptance—Finally, you will accept employment. Ideally, it will mark the beginning, or a _____, in your exciting and varied career. If you are like most Americans, you will change jobs for _____ during your work life. You will continue the process of self-assessment, research and decision-making in order to make effective and fulfilling changes.

Useful Expressions

Self-assessment is a vital and often **overlooked step** in planning your various career paths.
It is important to know who you are as a person.
This involves taking a careful inventory of your current career values, interests, skills and personal qualities.
Research—Online resources **are available to help you with** your preliminary information gathering.
Internships and part-time jobs are **an excellent way to** sample a field of interest.

They provide the opportunity to perform some of the job functions, observe others work and evaluate the environment.

Self-awareness, occupational awareness and intuition can all **play a part in** your decision-making.

Practice:

Choose the right word or phrase for each blank.

| investigating | involve | performing | evaluate |
| risk taking | positive | assessments | derive from |

1. He was shrewd in his personal _____.
2. Don't _____ a person on the basis of appearance.
3. A late booking may _____ you in extra cost.
4. These stories _____ his experiences during the Long March.
5. Police are still _____ how the accident happened.
6. A complex engine has many separate components, each _____ a different function.
7. The captain was not willing to _____ his ship through the straits in such bad weather.
8. Remember, keep a _____ attitude and good things will happen.

Resume Templates

Read the following hotel front desk resume template and answer the following questions.

a. What are the applicant's name and cell phone number?

b. What degree does the applicant have?

c. What was the applicant's major?

d. What are the job titles of the applicant's main work experience?

e. When was the applicant awarded Employee of the Month four times for positive attitude and attention to detail?

Resume Template

Leah Squire

Home: 123-555-6446 Cell: 123-555-9653

lsquire@email.com

125 East Street

Springfield, IL 62705

Education

Bachelor of Arts, **Springfield University,** Springfield, IL, May 2013

Major: English

Minor: Environmental Studies
Overall GPA 3.6; Honors each semester
Study Abroad: Madrid, Spain - Spring 2009

Springfield River High School, Springfield, IL, May 2008

Experience

Dining Hall Assistant, **Springfield University**, Springfield, IL
Fall 2012—present

- Perform preparatory work for Dining Hall chefs, including preparing fruits and vegetables, cleaning appliances, and organizing kitchen at the beginning and end of each day.
- Interact with hundreds of customers daily, serving breakfast, lunch, and dinner.
- Was awarded Employee of the Month twice for focus and attention to detail.

Administrative Aide, Wilson Physical Therapy Group, West way, IL
Summer 2011

- Responsible for interacting with dozens of clients on the phone daily.
- Managed clients' appointments and doctors' schedules using an online scheduling program.

Waiter, Mabel's Bar and Grille, Springfield, IL
Summer 2010—Summer 2011

- Took orders of up to one hundred customers daily.
- Responsible for assisting customers on the phone, placing take-out orders and answering general questions.
- Was awarded Employee of the Month four times for positive attitude and attention to detail.

Other Experience

- Member of Springfield River High School Culinary Club, Fall 2007—Spring 2008.
- Lead alto saxophone player in Springfield River High School Band, Fall 2007—Spring 2008.

Practice:

According to the template above, write a resume for yourself. Invent some qualifications and work experience. Then take turns to ask each other questions.

Example: A: What professional qualifications do you have?

B: I have a two-year diploma in hotel management.

A: What was your first job?

B: When I left college I worked in the Hilton Hotel.

Vocabulary

adaptability	[əˌdæptə'bɪləti]	n.	适应性，合用性
articulate	[ɑː'tɪkjuleɪt]	v.	清楚地发音，表达
bachelor	['bætʃələ]	n.	学士
client	['klaɪənt]	n.	顾客，客户
counsel	['kaʊnsl]	v.	提供咨询，建议
counselor	['kaʊnsələ]	n.	顾问，指导老师
evaluate	[ɪ'væljueɪt]	v.	评价
evaluation	[ɪˌvæljʊ'eɪʃn]	n.	估价
externship	['ekstɜːnʃɪp]	n.	校外实习期
frustration	[frʌ'streɪʃn]	n.	挫败，失意
identify	[aɪ'dentɪfaɪ]	v.	识别，确认
internship	['ɪntɜːnʃɪp]	n.	实习
inventory	['ɪnvəntri]	n.	清查，清单
investigate	[ɪn'vestɪgeɪt]	v.	调查，研究
milestone	['maɪlstəʊn]	n.	里程碑
overlook	[ˌəʊvə'lʊk]	v.	忽视，不予理会
perspective	[pə'spektɪv]	n.	看法，观点
preliminary	[prɪ'lɪmɪnəri]	adj.	起初的
preparatory	[prɪ'pærətri]	adj.	预备的，准备的
prioritize	[praɪ'ɒrətaɪz]	v.	按重要性排列，划分优先顺序
qualification	[ˌkwɒlɪfɪ'keɪʃn]	n.	资格
resume	[rɪ'zjuːm]	n.	履历
sample	['sɑːmpl]	v.	取样，抽样调查
suitability	[ˌsjuːtə'bɪləti]	n.	合适，适合
thoroughly	['θʌrəli]	adv.	彻底地，仔细认真地
trait	[treɪt]	n.	特点，特征
unrealistic	[ˌʌnrɪə'lɪstɪk]	adj.	不切实际的
vital	['vaɪtl]	adj.	至关重要的，必须的
alto saxophone			中音萨克斯
decision making			做决定
derive from			由……起源，取自
interact with			与……互动
risk-taking			冒险
self-awareness			自我意识
self-assessment			自我评估

take-out	外卖
job searching	找工作
pros and cons	利弊，优缺点

Exercises

I. Please translate the following sentences:
1. 本人接受英文教育，同时略通西班牙文。
2. 本人曾在某一公司担任推销员，前后有五年之久。
3. 两年前，自从离校后，在格兰酒店担任出纳员。
4. 我工作很有条理，办事效率高。
5. 随函附寄简历表一份，望能通知能否有机会见面。
6. I am a graduate of Hong Kong University, and have in addition the M. A. degree from UCLA.
7. I'm a highly-motivated and reliable person with excellent health and pleasant personality.
8. I have the ability to deal with personnel at all levels effectively.
9. I have good and extensive social connections.
10. If you desire an interview, I shall be most happy to come on any day and at any time you may appoint.

II. Discussion: Discuss the following topics in your group, then share your opinions in class:
1. How to deal with annoying coworkers?
2. How to turn workplace negativity into positive change?
3. What shouldn't you do when you start a new job?
4. Why do you need strong problem solving skills?
5. Why strong organizational skills are important for your career?

III. Writing: In addition to a resume, job advertisements often need a covering letter to highlight the applicant's best qualities. Please write a covering letter with some of the qualifications and skills for Catering & Hospitality jobs listed below.

- Positive attitude
- Willing to serve others
- Polite and friendly
- Good communication skills
- Excellent grooming standards
- Flexibility to respond to a range of different work situations
- Planning well so each event runs smoothly
- Managing your food and beverage team
- Good communication skills to find out exactly what your clients want
- Excellent organizational and administrative skills

- A cool head to deal with last minute requests and problems
- Knowledge of Food Hygiene Regulations
- Personal charm to greet organizers, hosts and VIPs and to show clients you are giving them full attention
- Experience with cash handling

How Can You Make Your CV More Effective?

Understanding Your Audience

As your personal marketing campaign, your CV must make the reader believe you're a worthwhile product. Business people generally have the same objectives: profit, bigger market share, developing their business and creating new products for their customers. They will look for candidates who will help them to achieve these objectives.

Identifying an Achievement

Try to pick at least one specific example per job you've held and explain briefly how it improved the business. Always keep examples relevant to the role you are applying for.

Personal achievements are also valuable pieces to include as they often show focus and commitment that will impress recruiters. But be careful not to give valuable space to insignificant achievements.

Avoiding Alienation

Be very careful of using abbreviations, especially if you're changing industry. The first person who evaluates your CV is usually somebody in the HR team who may not be an expert in your field. They will be given a rundown of requirements to mark CVs against, so statements like "extensive experience in working with QCIs" may mean nothing to them, even if it's an impressive skill that means you could do the job with your hands tied behind your back.

Skills for All Occasions

There are countless transferable skills that can be used for many jobs in many companies. If you're looking to change industry, remember that, although an employer may not need your skills on a certain IT package, they may be impressed that you have the ability to pick up new software quickly.

Alternative CVs

Technology has made everyone's life easier when it comes to recruitment. From uploading your CV to an online database so employers can pick out your skills, to recording a video CV that gives employers a visual overview of what you can offer to their companies, your only limitation is your own creativity.

Dialogue-Dialogue-Scripts & Reference Answer

Part 1　The Front Desk　前厅服务英语

Brainstorm Answers:

people: reservationist, bellman, doorman, guests, receptions, cashiers …
place: entrance, lobby, front office, reception area, front desk, registration desk …
things: luggage, registration form, passport, room card, telephone, computers, luggage van, cash, credit cards …
services: bell service, reservation service, reception service …

Scene One　Room Reservations

I. Activities

1. FIT Reservation

Dialogue-Scripts:

Scene: Ryan Burt, who works in Seattle, is going to have a business trip to China. Now Mr. Burt is making a reservation at Shangri-la Hotel in Changzhou through a long distance call.

(R=Receptionist, C=Customer)

R: Good morning, Shangri-la Hotel. May I help you?
C: Good morning. I'd like to book a room from July 13th to 15th. Have you got vacancies then? I'd like to make a reservation for three nights.
R: All right, sir. Would you like to have a single room or a double room?
C: Single room, please.
R: Let me check … yes, we have a single room available.
C: With bath or without?
R: It's a single room with a bathtub and toilet.
C: That sounds good. Is there free wifi inside the guest room?
R: Certainly, sir. It's easy to get online in your room with the password of our hotel. And with a high speed.
C: What is the room rate per night?
R: Let me see … a single room is RMB 668 yuan per night.
C: Does it include breakfast?
R: Yes, it includes a simple breakfast in lounge bar on the second floor.
C: Well, that's perfect. By the way, do you accept Mastercard?

R: Yes, we do. What time will you be arriving?

C: I should be there at around 5 p.m. on the 13th.

R: OK, sir. May I have your name and contact number, please?

C: Yes, my name is Ryan Burt. My phone number is 206-737-3628.

R: Would you please spell your name?

C: Ryan Burt, R-Y-A-N, B-U-R-T.

R: Mr. Ryan Burt. A single room with bathtub and air conditioning for the nights from July13th to 15th, including breakfast. Am I correct?

C: Yes, that's right. Thank you.

R: You are welcome, sir. We are looking forward to your arriving. Goodbye!

C: Thank you. Goodbye!

Answers:

DEMO. COPY	For Registration Call 0519-****-****
RESERVATION SLIP	
Reservation # 1	Enquiry Date: 05 / 26 / 20** (Month) (Date) (Year)
Arrival Date: 06/13/20**	Departure Date:
Guest's Name: Ryan Burt	
Room # 203	Facilities: bathtub, air-conditioning wifi, with breakfast
Floor: 2nd Floor	
Room Type:	
No. of Beds: Single	
Prepared by: 1 Manager:	Enquirer:

Practice: 略

2. Group Reservation

Dialogue-Scripts:

Scene: The telephone rings. The receptionist answers the phone.

(R=Receptionist, C=Customer)

R: Good afternoon. Grand Hotel, reservations. May I help you?

C: Yes. I am calling from San Diego Green Farm Company. I'd like to know if you have rooms available in early November this winter. We are going to have a business conference in Shanghai.

R: May I know how many people in your group for the conference?

C: 24 people totally.

R: What kind of room would you like, sir?

C: I'd like 4 single rooms with double beds and 10 twin rooms. And we plan to stay here from November 3rd to 6th.

R: Ok. Please wait for a moment, sir. Let me see … sorry sir, I'm afraid that we can only confirm 2 single rooms with double beds, but we have more twin rooms with rear views for those days.

C: Oh, so let me think … what is the price difference?

R: A single room with a double bed is RMB 489 per night and the twin room is 465.

C: It sounds normally the same. So I will choose one more twin room instead. Is there any special rate for a group reservation?

R: Yes, there is a 12 percent discount.

C: That's great.

R: By the way, how will you settle the accounts, please?

C: Our company will cover all the expenses and we will send you a cheque soon.

R: Thank you, sir. Is there anything else I can do for you?

C: No, thank you.

R: Ok. Let me confirm the details with you, sir. 2 single rooms with double beds and 11 twin rooms from November 3rd to 6th. The group is San Diego Green Farm Company. Is that correct?

C: Yes, it's great. Thank you.

R: My pleasure. Looking forward to serving you, sir. Have a nice day!

Answers:

a. San Diego Green Farm Company.

b. 24 people totally. They will come to the hotel on November 3rd and stay until 6th.

c. They need 4 single rooms with double beds and 10 twin rooms. Then they changed into 2 single rooms with double beds and 11 twin rooms.

d. Yes, there is a 12 percent discount.

e. The company will pay for all the expenses. They will send a cheque soon.

Practice:

FIT reservation is more flexible, more convenient, no need to wait, but usually pays higher room rate; Group reservation needs to make the confirmation to see if there is enough rooms with narrow choices, but usually has discounts.

3. Reservation Revision

Dialogue-Scripts:

Dialogue A:

The guest May made a room reservation for 3 nights. She wants to extend her stay for 5 nights. The hotel clerk helps her revise the reservation.

Clerk: Room Reservations. May I help you?

May: Good afternoon. My name is May, and I have made a reservation in Holiday Inn for 3 nights from February 8th to 10th. I'd like to extend my staying here for 2 more nights until the 12th.

Clerk: For 5 nights from February 8th to February 12th?

May: That's right.

Clerk: Is there any change in your room type? You reserved a double room with a double bed.

May: No.

Clerk: Thank you, madam. We will extend the reservation for you.

Dialogue B:

(Marisa, an agent from Youth Travel Agency, has booked 15 rooms in Sunrise Hotel in the name of the agency. But due to the new traveling schedule, she is calling the hotel to alter the reservation)

Clerk: Good morning. Sunrise Hotel. How can I help you?

Marisa: Yes. This is Marisa calling from Canada. I have to change the date of the reservation.

Clerk: Ok. Would you please tell me in whose name has the reservation been made?

Marisa: Yes. It's in the name of the company called "Youth Travel Agency".

Clerk: Ok. Let me check ... you've booked 15 twin rooms for September 15th to 17th, right?

Marisa: Right. And is it possible for us to postpone the reservation dates to be September 21st to 23rd?

Clerk: Please wait for a minute, let me check ... yes, we have enough twin rooms available for those days.

Marisa: That's perfect!

Clerk: So, you book 15 twin rooms from September 21st to 23rd, in the name of "Youth Travel Agency", is that correct?

Marisa: Yes, it is. Thanks a lot!

Clerk: It's my pleasure. Have a nice day!

Answers:

a. Room Reservations

   for 3 nights from February 8th to 10th

   For 5 nights from February 8th to February 12th

   room type

   We will extend the reservation for you

b. How can I help you

   Would you please tell me in whose name has the reservation been made

   15 twin rooms

   we have enough twin rooms available for those days

   It's my pleasure

Practice: 略

4. Over-booking

Dialogue-Scripts:

Alice is calling New Asian Hotel to reserve a double room. The reservation clerk is answering the phone.

Clerk: Good morning, New Asian Hotel. Reservations. May I help you?
Alice: I'd like to book a triple room for June 13th.
Clerk: Just a moment, please … sorry, I'm afraid our hotel is fully booked for that day. You know it is the popular season for the seaside summer festival here. Is it possible for you to change the reservation date?
Alice: Oh, no. We will come to attend a very important conference in another hotel nearby. And that hotel has been fully booked already. That's a great pity!
Clerk: I'm very sorry. I will put you on our waiting list and call you if there is a cancellation.
Alice: That's very kind of you. But could you recommend another hotel nearby to me?
Clerk: In this case, I would suggest that you try Green Forest Inn. They usually have a large number of triple rooms for the young people who have package tour here. The telephone number is 67898868.
Alice: Thank you so much. I really appreciate your help!
Clerk: Thank you for calling us. Goodbye!

Answers:

I'm afraid our hotel is fully booked for that day
to change the reservation date
I will put you on our waiting list and call you if there is a cancellation
67898868
Thank you for calling us

Practice: 略

II. Exercise

Translations

1. Would you like to have a single room or a double room?
2. May I know how many people in your group for the conference?
3. There is a 20 percent discount in this month.
4. How will you settle the accounts, please?
5. I will put you on our waiting list and call you if there is a cancellation.
6. 我来看下……是的，我们有单人间提供。

7. 您可以更改预订日期吗?
8. 单人间每晚698元。
9. 您应该付1200元的押金。
10. 抱歉我们酒店那天已经订满了。

Role-play: 略

Correct order: 8→3→6→2→5→1→4→7。

Scene Two At the Reception Desk

I. Activities

1. Early Check-in

Dialogue-Scripts:

(R= Receptionist, G=Guest)

R: Good morning, sir. How are you today?

G: Fine, thank you. I just arrive at the hotel and I have a reservation in the name of Tom Brown.

R: Mr Tom Brown?

G: Yes. I reserved a single room online the day before yesterday.

R: Please wait for a minute. Let me check for you … so you are staying with us for 2 nights, right?

G: Yes, that's right.

R: I'm sorry, Mr Tom Brown. Your room isn't quite ready yet. Normally our check-in is from 3 p.m.

G: Yes, I knew that when I made reservation online. But my flight arrived early this morning.

R: I'm sorry but Housekeeping are still cleaning your room now.

G: God! So what should I do now? You see, I can't go anywhere with two pieces of luggage now and I am really tired after a long time trans-ocean flight.

R: Well, you are welcome to store your luggage with us. May I suggest you have a cup of coffee and relax in our Lobby Lounge? I'll come and get you when your room is ready. Is that ok for you?

G: Ok. How long will that be?

R: I'll ask Housekeeping to do your room as quickly as possible.

G: Thank you. I need to fresh up before my meeting this afternoon. By the way, where is your Lobby Lounge?

R: Please go around the corner and turn left. It's at the back of the lobby.

G: Thank you.

Answers:

a. He reserved online the day before yesterday.

b. He wants a single room for 2 nights.

c. Normal check-in is from 3 p.m.

d. Because the Housekeeping are still cleaning his room now.

e. The receptionist suggests him store his luggage with them and have a cup of coffee and relax in the Lobby Lounge.

f. He can go around the corner and turn left.

Practice:

a. I'm sorry, your room isn't quite ready yet.

b. Normally our check-in time is 3 p.m.

c. I'm sorry but Housekeeping are still cleaning your room.

d. I'm afraid that we don't have any rooms ready at the moment.

2. Extending the Stay

Dialogue-Scripts:

(R= Receptionist, G=Guest)

R: Good morning, Mrs Miller. May I help you?

G: Morning. I'd like to extend our stay for one more night. You know it's the first time for our family to come to Dalian, and it's a great seaside city. We don't want to lose the chance to attend the Seafood Festival tomorrow.

R: Certainly, Mrs Miller. It's very popular with a good selection of fresh seafood in this summer time. Please wait for a minute. Let me check it in the computer.

G: Sure. Thank you. I cannot wait to try the seafood tomorrow.

R: I see. One of your two rooms that you are staying in has been registered by a business group for tonight, I mean room 3834. Would you mind transferring to the room 3805? It's the nearest one on the same floor.

G: That's ok. I'll take it.

R: By the way, the rate is 380 yuan higher because it's a business room with a king bed instead of the queen bed.

G: No problem. When can we change rooms?

R: Well, the guest in this room will check out at 11:00 am and I will inform you then.

G: Sounds great. It's very kind of you. Thank you!

R: You are welcome.

Answers:

> **Dalian Seaside Beach Hotel**
>
> Guest's Name: *Susan Miller*
> Room Number: *3832, 3805*
> Check-in Date: *Aug. 4*
> Check-out Date: *Aug. 7*
> Rate: *1250yuan*
> Room Type: *Business Room*
> Bed: *king bed*

practice:

Procedures of extending the stay:

1. Greetings.
2. Ask the guest about room number, name, the extending time, room type, room amount etc.
3. Check the computer record to check the room availability.
4. Make the confirmation with the guest.
5. Ask the guest the way of payment and make a record in the computer.
6. Extend the wishes to the guest.

3. Changing the Room

Dialogue-Scripts:

(R= Receptionist, G=Guest)

R: Good morning, madam. Is there anything I can do for you?

G: Yes. I'd like to change my room.

R: Is there anything wrong with your room?

G: I want to change my room to a quiet one, because I cannot sleep well last night. The room I'm staying in is near the entrance of the elevator and it's so noisy at night. More than that, it smells of smoke.

R: I'm very sorry to hear that, madam. Some guests unfortunately ignore the Non-smoking signs. May I know your name and your room number?

G: Sally Taylor from room 1021.

R: Ok, Ms Taylor. Do you want the same type of room?

G: Yes, a single room with a double bed, please.

R: I see. Please wait for a moment, I will check the computer for you. There is a single room on the 13th floor and it's at the corner. The room rate is same. would you want this one?

G: Yes, I will take it.

R: The room number is 1349. Would you please fill in this room - change form?

G: Sure. Here it is. And this is my room card.

R: Thank you, madam. Here is your new room card. You can come to your new room right now.

G: It's very kind of you. Thank you.

R: My pleasure. Hope you enjoy your stay in our hotel.

Answers:

Is there anything I can do, I cannot sleep well last night, the entrance of the elevator, noisy, smoke, 1021, a single, a double, 13th, at the corner, room changing form, Hope you enjoy your stay in our hotel.

Practice: 5→3→1→4→6→2→7

Greet the guest.

Get to know the guest's room number.

Check the computer record to find the room availability.

If there is a room available, change the room for the guest and make a record of the changing information.

Ask the guest to fill in the room changing form.

Confirm the guest about room changing details including name, time, room type and room number.

Extend your best wishes.

III. Exercise

Translations:

1. I'm sorry, Mr Brown. Your room isn't quite ready yet. Normally our check-in is from 2 p.m.
2. One of your two rooms has been registered by a tour group for tonight. Would you mind transferring to the room 4039?
3. By the way, the rate is 300 yuan higher because it's a double room with a king bed.
4. I'll ask Housekeeping to do your room as quickly as possible.
5. Here is your new room card and you can come to your new room right now.
6. 很抱歉，客房部现在正打扫您的房间。
7. 您可以把行李寄存在我们这里。
8. 我可以建议您去我们的咖啡吧 (coffee bar) 里喝杯咖啡，休息一下吗？
9. 这间房的客人10点钟结账，到时候我会通知您。
10. 请问您住的房间有什么问题吗？

Role-play: 略

Discussion:

a. Greeted, registered, and assigned rooms to guests.

b. Operated the switchboard.

c. Answered telephone or personal queries related to hotel services and resolved any issues.

d. Processed guests check-in and check-out.

e. Prepared and completed room and restaurant bills.

f. Assisted guests in storing valuables in secure deposit box.

g. Liaised with other departments of hotel.

h. Handled payments through cash, checks and credit cards.

Scene Three — Business Center

I. Activities

1. Ticket booking

Dialogue-Scripts:

Scene: A guest is coming to the business center and asking for help.

(C=Clerk, G=Guest)

G: Good Morning. Could you do me a favor?

C: Certainly, sir. What can I do for you?

G: I want to book an air ticket from Shanghai to Sanya on October 8th.

C: Please wait for a moment. I will check on my computer. … There are three flights available that day. One is at 9:50 in the morning and the other two are at 3:50 and 5:50 in the afternoon. What time is suitable for you, morning or afternoon?

G: It's better in the morning. Does the flight at 9:50 depart from Shanghai Pudong International Airport?

C: Let me see. Yes, sir. It will depart from Shanghai Pudong International Airport at 9:50 a.m. and arrive at Sanya Phoenix International Airport at 12:55 p.m. And it's offered by China Eastern Airlines. Will this be all right?

G: Yes, that would be nice. Pudong International airport is very convenient for me because it's nearby.

C: You are right, sir. How do you want your ticket, first class, business class or economy class?

G: Business class, please.

C: And how many tickets do you want?

G: Just for me.

C: Would you please show me your passport to make the reservation?

G: Sure. Here you are. How much is the air ticket?

C: It shows RMB 2840 altogether. How would you like to pay, sir?

G: I will pay by my credit card.

C: That's fine! We will give you the ticket in two or three days. Will you come to pick up your ticket or should we send it to your room?

G: It will be great to send it to my room. Thank you!

C: My pleasure! Have a pleasant day!

Answers:

a. F   b. F   c. T   d. F   e. T   f. F

Practice:

1. g   2. b   3. a   4. d   5. e   6. h   7. i   8. f   9. c

2. Renting Equipment

Dialogue-Scripts:

(C=Clerk, G=Guest)

C: Good morning, madam. Is there anything I can do for you?

G: Yes, please. I'd like to rent a laptop tonight.

C: Certainly, madam. For how long, please?

G: Just one night. I need to prepare for a business report tonight.

C: No problem, madam. Which brand do you prefer? We have a great selection of large sized laptops in the center, you see, like Levono, IBM, Toshiba or Dell. We also have tablets, too.

G: Well, I need a larger size which is comfortable to use. May I have a look, please?

C: Sure. … Here they are. Which one do you like?

G: I want to rent this one, Toshiba.

C: Great. This is a new one in good condition. Here is the rental form and the instructions. Please read the details carefully and fill in the rental form.

G: OK. So how about the charge?

C: The charge is 15 yuan an hour. And you need to pay 2000 yuan as a deposit in advance.

G: No problem.

C: Could you show me your room card, please?

G: Here you are. By the way, is there broadband or WiFi in the room? I need to work online.

C: Yes, madam. We do have free WiFi in all our rooms, and here is our network name and WiFi password.

G: Wonderful. Thank you for your help.

C: You are welcome, madam. Have a nice day!

Answers:

rent a laptop, Just one night, Which brand do you prefer, large sized, tablets, Which one do you like, Toshiba, 15 yuan, 2000 yuan, broadband, WiFi, network name, WiFi password.

practice:

The procedures of renting equipment in the business center:

1. Greet the guest warmly and politely.
2. Make sure the kinds of equipment the guest wants to rent.
3. Ask how long the guest wants to keep it.
4. Help guest to find out the equipment and explain the rentals to the guest.
5. Ask the guest to fill in the rental form with his/her identification.
6. Explain the rental fee and ask the guest to pay the deposit in advance.
7. Try to answer the guest's questions and extend the wishes.

3. Interpretation Service

Dialogue-Scripts:

(C=Clerk, G=Guest)

C: Good afternoon, Mr Black. How is your day going?
G: Very fine, thank you. I'd like to ask you for help to find a Germany interpreter for me.
C: Certainly, sir. Do you have any special requirements?
G: The interpreter must understand biology terminology and have the experience of business negotiation.
C: When will you need the interpreter?
G: It's better for the interpreter to come to see me no later than tomorrow noon. We need to talk and discuss in details in advance.
C: Ok. I need to contact the translation company first, for there isn't any suitable Germany interpreter for you in our hotel.
G: Great, thank you for that. What's the price for the service?
C: 500 yuan per hour.
G: That's fine.
C: Would you like to charge it to your room directly?
G: That will be great. When will you get back to me?
C: I will inform you as soon as we find one for you.
G: I see. Thank you so much!
C: It's my pleasure.

Answers:

a. Germany interpreter.
b. The interpreter must understand biology terminology and have the experience of business negotiation.
c. No later than tomorrow noon.
d. 500 yuan per hour.
e. The service fee will be charged to his room directly.

Practice:

a. Seven languages: English, Spanish, Italian, French, Russian, Japanese, and Arabic.

b. 72 hours.

c. 2000 yuan.

d. No, it doesn't.

e. The guest can contact the hotel for the service both by calling the business center or sending email to them.

III. Exercise

Translations:

1. There are four flights available on May 13th. What time is suitable for you, morning or afternoon?
2. Will you come to pick up your ticket or should we send it to your room?
3. Here is the rental form and the instructions. Please read the details carefully and fill in the form.
4. We have free WiFi in all our rooms, and here is our network name and WiFi password.
5. We have a great selection of tablets in the center, like iPad, Samsung, Lenovo, Dell and Toshiba.
6. 费用是每小时30元，您需要提前付3000元定金。
7. 我要先联系一下翻译公司，因为我们酒店没有合适的意大利语翻译提供给您。
8. 费用是每天900元。您想直接记在您的房账上吗？
9. 我们找到翻译后会尽快通知您。
10. 您想选择哪种机票，头等舱，商务舱还是经济舱？

Role-play: 略

Discussion:

1. Guest's name and room number, when/where to go, what kind of ticket, how many tickets, any special requirements, etc.
2. Hard/soft seat, hard/soft berth, one way, round trip, first class, business class, ecumenic class, etc.
3. The guest's name, contact number, what kind of equipment, ask guest to fill the rental form and read the instructions, pay deposit in advance.
4. Yes, there are more and more business conferences hold in higher level hotels now and it's necessary to provide the service on it.
5. Depend on students' choices: train, ship, airplane, coach, bike, hike, etc.

Scene Four — Concierge Service

I. Activities

1. Pick-up Service

Dialogue-Scripts:

Scene: A hotel representative is coming to the airport to pick up a guest, holding a welcome board.

(C=Clerk, G=Guest)

G: Good Morning. Are you the clerk from Garden Hotel? I'm Eric Lord from Australia.

C: Oh, nice to meet you, Mr Lord. I'm Mary, the representative of Garden Hotel.

G: Nice to meet you, too.

C: Welcome to Chengdu, Mr Lord. I hope you had a good trip.

G: Yes, I had a really good trip this time. Thank you.

C: How many pieces of luggage do you have, Mr Lord?

G: Two.

C: Ok. Let me help you with your luggage here. The car is waiting outside the airport. We'll go to Garden Hotel at once. This way, please.

G: Ok. Thank you.

C: Here is our car. Please take care.

G: Thank you.

C: Is this your first trip to Chengdu?

G: Yes. I know it's famous for Giant Panda.

C: You are right, Mr Lord. You can visit Giant Panda Breeding Research Base which is the most popular place for foreigners. And also you can enjoy a day away from the city and experience the natural beauty of Qingcheng Mountain.

G: That sounds great. How can I get there? Are there any buses I can take?

C: Yes sir. You can take No.902 bus to Giant Panda Breeding Research Base and No. 101 bus to Qingcheng Mountain. Or you can take a taxi if you want.

G: I see. Thank you so much for your information.

C: You are welcome, sir.

(A few minutes later, at the gate of Garden Hotel)

C: Dear Mr Lord, we are arriving at Garden Hotel.

G: Oh, it looks very modern.

C: Your Room No. is 1635. Hope you'll have a nice trip here.

G: Thank you for all your help.

C: It's my pleasure.

Answers:

a. F   b. T   c. F   d. T   e. F   f. T

Practice:

a. It is located in the Beach area, 17 kilometers from the city centre and 29 kilometers from International Airport.

b. The guests staying in Suites, Villas and to our Gold card holders.

c. 120 RMB.

d. The hotel personnel will hold a printed placard saying "Blue Ocean Hotel welcome + your name" at the airport terminal.

e. The driver MUST show you a code that match your booking code (the hotel provides you with when confirming your booking).

2. Luggage Deposit

Dialogue-Scripts:

(C=Clerk, G=Guest)

C: Good morning. Concierge desk. May I help you?

G: Good morning. I'll be checking out very soon and I need to attend a meeting this morning. I am calling to find out if I can leave my luggage here for a while after I check out.

C: Please don't worry, madam. We can look after your luggage for you. When would you come back for it?

G: At around 5:00 this afternoon.

C: I see. May I have your name and your room number, please?

G: Yes. Sophia Gates. Room 505.

C: How many pieces of luggage do you have?

G: Two.

C: Ok, Ms Gates, we will arrange the bellman to Room 505 to pick up your luggage at once. Please don't forget to put your name tag on it.

G: Great. Is there a charge for that?

C: Well, for our guests, it's free for 24 hours. We will take good care of your luggage until 5:00 p.m. today. You can claim your luggage with your ID at our Concierge Desk in the lobby.

G: Thank you for your help.

C: You are welcome.

Answers:

Guest's Name: Sophia Gates

Room Number: 505

Luggage Amount: two

Pick-up time: 5:00 p.m. today

practice:

Swimming Pool | Laundry Service | Restroom | 24 hr Room Service

Shuttle Bus Service | Do Not Disturb Sign | Grocery Store | Fitting Room

3. Mail Delivery

Dialogue-Scripts:

(C=Clerk, G=Guest)

C: Good afternoon, sir. Is there anything I can do for you?
G: Good afternoon. I'd like to send an express mail to another city.
C: Certainly, sir. May I know what it is?
G: It's a brochure of our company.
C: I see. We offer two ways of delivery, one-day delivery and normal delivery which usually takes 3~5 days.
G: One-day delivery is better, because it's very urgent.
C: Ok. Please wait for a minute. Well, the charge is 50 yuan for your express mail with one-day delivery.
G: That's ok.
C: Would you please fill in this application form with your telephone number and your signature?
G: No problem.
C: Would you please show me your room card?
G: Here you are.
C: Thank you sir. Here is your bill. Would you like to pay in cash or would you like to charge it directly to your room?
G: Please go with my room charge.
C: Certainly, sir. I will call the Express Mail Service Company to get your mail immediately.

G: Thank you so much!

C: My pleasure. Have a nice day!

Answers:

send an express mail, one-day delivery, normal delivery, One-day delivery, 50 yuan, your telephone number, your signature, pay in cash, charge it directly to your room

Practice:

a. Greet the guests warmly and politely.

b. Understand the details of the requirement, and make a record of it.

c. Make clear the charge of the service.

d. Contact the relevant person who can deal with the services.

III. Exercise

Translations:

1. The car is waiting outside the airport. We'll go to the hotel at once.
2. You can enjoy a day away from the city and experience the natural beauty of Yellow Mountain.
3. You can take No.302 bus to the city center, or you can take a taxi if you want.
4. You can claim your luggage with your ID at our Concierge Desk in the lobby.
5. I will call the Express Mail Service Company to get your mail immediately.
6. 希望您的旅途非常顺利，我来帮您拿行李吧。
7. 这是您第一次来青岛吗？
8. 我们会看管好您的行李，请问您什么时候来取呢？
9. 我们马上安排行李员到2126房间取您的行李，请不要忘记在行李上放上您的名牌。
10. 请您填写一下这份申请表，附上您的电话号码，好吗？

Role-play: 略

Discussion:

a. limousine 豪华车   b. compact car 小型轿车   c. luggage van 行李车

d. sports car 跑车   e. jeep 吉普车   f. coach 大客车

g. SUV (Sport Utility Vehicle) 运动型多用途汽车

h. RV (Recreational Vehicle) 房车

i. cabriolet 敞篷车

Scene Five — The Cashier

I. Activities

1. Credit Card Payment

Dialogue-Scripts:

Scene: A guestis going to check out in Grand Hotel.

(C=Cashier, G=Guest)

G: Morning. I'd like to check out, please.

C: Good morning, sir. May I know your name and room number, please?

G: I'm Peter Singh. Room 1340. Here is my room card.

C: Thank you, Mr Singh. Have you used the mini-bar or other services this morning?

G: No.

C: OK. Mr. Singh. Please wait for a moment, I'll print the bill for you. …Here is your bill. It totals RMB 1209, including a 10% service charge. Please have a check.

G: Yes, it's correct. But I don't have enough cash for it. May I pay by my credit card?

C: Yes, we do accept some major credit cards, such as American Express, Visa or MasterCard. What card do you have?

G: Visa Card.

C: Thank you. Would you please sign your name here, Mr Singh?

G: OK... Here you are.

C: Thank you. Please take your credit card and keep the receipt. We hope you will be staying with us again.

G: Thank you very much. Goodbye.

Answers:

a. F   b. T   c. F   d. T   e. F   f. F

Practice:

a. Alipay (支付宝)
b. Visa (维萨卡)
c. MasterCard (万事达卡)
d. Diners Clube International (大莱信用卡)
e. WeChat Pay (微信支付)
f. UnionPay (中国银联卡)

2. Cash Payment

Dialogue-Scripts:

(C=Cashier, G=Guest)

C: Good morning, madam. Can I help you?

G: Yes, please. I'd like to settle my bill.

C: Certainly, madam. Which room, please?

G: 3236. Mrs. Simon.

C: May I have your key card, please?

G: Sure. Here it is.

C: Thank you. Please wait for a minute, Mrs Simon. I'll draw up your bill for you.

G: Thank you.

C: Here you are. It totals RMB 1870. Please would you like to check it.

G: That's correct.

C: How will you settle your account?

G: In cash.

C: May I have the receipt of your deposit?

G: Oh, here you are.

C: Thank you. You paid a deposit of RMB 2000. Here is your invoice and your change, 130 yuan.

G: Thank you very much.

C: You are welcome, Mrs Simon. Have a nice day!

Answers:

a. Mrs. Simon from room 3236.

b. "May I have your key card, please?"

c. The bill totals RMB 1870.

d. The guest will pay in cash.

e. The deposit is RMB 2000 yuan and the change is 130 yuan.

practice:

Same Steps:

In both ways of payment, the cashier has to ask the name and the room number of the guest, ask guest to give back the room card, explain the total amount, ask the way to pay and give back the receipt or invoice to the guest.

Different Steps:

Credit card payment: the cashier needs to ask and make sure the credit card can be used in the hotel and ask the guest to sign the name.

Cash payment: the cashier needs to ask for the deposit slip and give back the change.

3. Foreign Currency Exchange

Dialogue-Scripts:

(C=Cashier, G=Guest)

C: Good morning, sir. Can I help you?
G: Yes. Can I change some Chinese Renminbi here?
C: Certainly, sir. What kind of foreign currency have you got, sir?
G: US dollars. What's the exchange rate today?
C: According to today's exchange rate, one dollar is equivalent to 6.36 yuan. How much would you like to change, sir?
G: 300 dollars. Here is the money.
C: May I see your passport, please?
G: Here you are.
C: Now here is the exchange memo for you. Please fill in this form with your passport number, your name, the total amount and your room number.
G: Sure.
C: And please sign your name here.
G: Is that all right?
C: Yes, that's good. Here is 1908 yuan for you. Please have a check and keep the exchange memo.
G: By the way, what should I do with the remaining Renminbi?
C: You can go to several specialized foreign exchange banks to change it back, like Bank of China, China Construction Bank, Industrial and Commercial Bank of China, or you can go to the airport exchange office, too.
G: I see. Thank you for your information.
C: That's my pleasure.

Answers:

Chinese RMB (Renminbi), US dollars, 6.36 yuan, 300 dollars, exchange memo, passport number, name, total amount, room number, 1908 yuan, exchange office.

Practice: 略

III. Exercise

Translations:

1. Yes, we do accept some major credit cards, such as American Express, Visa or MasterCard.
2. May I have your key card, please? I'll draw up your bill for you.
3. You paid a deposit of RMB 1500. Here is your invoice and your change, 68 yuan.
4. According to today's exchange rate, one dollar is equivalent to 6.36 yuan.
5. You can go to the Bank of China to change it back, or you can go to the airport ex-

change office, too.

6. 请稍等，我为您打印账单。
7. 您打算如何结账呢？
8. 先生，请问您想兑换什么外币呢？
9. 先生，请问您想兑换多少呢？
10. 这是您的兑换税单，请您检查一下。

Role-play: 略

Complete the dialogue:

Certainly, sir. May I know your name and your room number, please?

Here is your bill, Ms. Williams. Your bill totals RMB 1089 yuan. Please have a check.

How will you settle your account?

Would you please show me your card?

Would you please sign your name here?

Here is your invoice and your credit card. Please keep them. We hope you will be staying with us again.

Part 2 Housekeeping Department 客房服务英语

Brainstorm Answers:

- people: room attendant, housekeeper, cleaner, inspector, laundry attendant …
- places: guest room, public area, laundry department …
- things: bed sheet, bed cover, quilt, pillow, towel, hanger, body lotion, shampoo, soap, shower cap, hair dryer, slipper, toothbrush, robe, blanket, bedside phone, desk lamp, glass cup, mini-bar, in-room safe, kettle, television, air conditioner, High Speed of Wireless & Wired Internet Access, laundry, laundry list, laundry bag, charge, dry-cleaning, washing, ironing …
- services: chamber service, cleaning, laundry service, express service …

Scene One — Chamber Service

I. Activities

1. Cleaning the Room

Dialogue-Scripts:

Scene: The housekeeping comes to clean the guest's room.

(H=Housekeeping, G=Guest)

H: Good morning, Housekeeping. I've come to clean your room.

G: Come in, please.

H: May I clean your room now?

G: Yes, I'm going out.

H: It's raining outside now, there is an umbrella in your closet.

G: Oh, nice. Thanks.

H: Do you need fresh sheets?

G: No, the sheets will be OK for another night.

H: Do you need new towels?

G: No, the towels are OK as well.

H: OK. Is there anything you do need?

G: Yes, I need a new toilet roll. By the way, could you get me a flask of hot water. I need some hot water to wash down my medicine.

H: Of course, anything else?

G: Yes, some shampoo and conditioner, please.

H: It's getting cold, do you need extra covers?

G: That would be great. I was about to ask.

H: OK. I will go and get them. I will vacuum your room and make your bed later.

G: OK, thanks.

Answers:

a. A new toilet roll, a flask of hot water, shampoo, conditioner and extra covers.

b. In the closet.

c. A flask of hot water.

d. Yes, he does.

e. She will vacuum the room and make the bed.

Practice: 2→5→3→7→4→1→6

2. Turn-down Service

Dialogue-Scripts:

Scene: The housekeeper comes to do the turn-down service for the guest.

(H=Housekeeper, G=Guest)

H: Good evening, madam and sir. May I do the turn-down service for you now?

G: Oh, thank you. But you see, we are having some friends over. We're going to have a small party here in the room. Could you come back in three hours?

H: Certainly, madam. I'll let the overnight staff know. They will come then.

G: That's fine. Well, our friends seem to be a little late. Would you tidy up a bit in the bathroom? I've just taken a bath and it is quite messy now. Also, please bring us a bottle of boiled water. We'd like to treat our friends to typical Chinese tea.

H: Yes, madam. I'll bring in some fresh towels together with boiled water.

G: OK.

H: Do you need anything extra for your friends?

G: Yeah. that would be nice, and a small table if you could.

H: If your friends would like to stay overnight, please let me know and I can book rooms for them!

G: No, they will leave tonight, thanks.

H: (Having done all on request)
   It's growing dark. Would you like me to draw the curtains for you, sir and madam?

G: Why not? That would be so cozy.

H: May I turn on the lights for you?

G: Yes, please. I'd like to do some reading while waiting.

H: Yes, madam. When your friends arrive, the bellman will guide them to your room. Is there anything else I can do for you?

G: No more. You've been a great help. Thank you very much.

H: You're welcome. Goodbye, and do have a very pleasant evening.

Answers:

1. T   2. F   3. T   4. F   5. F   6. T   7. T

Practice:

Turn-down service is usually offered between 5 p.m. and 8 p.m. The room attendant will take away the bed cover, take a quilt corner by the telephone side, fold it into triangle and place the pillow properly. Also, the curtain would be drawn close, the bedside lamp would be turned on. In one word, turn-down service aims to make the guest feel like at home. An item of confectionery such as a chocolate or a mint is typically left on top of a pillow in the bed that has been turned down. Some hotels have more elaborate turn-down services, such as bed-time stories for children and cocktails served to young couples.

3. Adding Beds

Dialogue-Scripts:

Scene: A guest is calling room center for an extra bed.

(R=Receptionist, G=Guest)

R: Good afternoon. Room center. Anna speaking. How can I help you?

G: Good afternoon, this is Mrs. Evans in room 2008. My daughter will be staying with me tonight, so I need an extra bed in my room.

R: OK. We can bring up a fold-out bed for you, madam.

G: Thank you. My daughter is bringing her baby, so I will also need a cot.

R: That's no problem. May I know how old the baby is so as to provide the exact cot?

G: The baby is one year old.

R: We have the right size cot for the baby.

G: Can you put some extra blankets in my wardrobe.

R: Yes, of course.

G: Will you bring sheets and bedding for the extra bed?

R: Yes, of course.

G: How much should I pay for those?

R: The extra bed is RMB500 yuan per night while others are free. The charge will be billed to your room account. The bellman will send the bill for you to sign in 10 minutes. Will that be all right?

G: All right.

R: Do you need extra towels and baby shampoo?

G: Yes, please.

R: Is there anything else I can help with?

G: Could you please make sure no one disturbs us so the baby can sleep well?

R: Certainly, no one will disturb you, madam. Anything else, madam?

G: Nothing else. Thank you very much.

R: You're welcome. We are always at your service.

Answers:

in room 2008

an extra bed

need a cot

so as to provide the exact cot

some extra blankets

sheets and bedding

billed to your room account

extra towels and baby shampoo

no one disturbs us

Practice:

After being told to add a bed, the room attendant should:

a. check to ensure that the bed or cot is in good condition.

b. prepare bed sheet, blanket, pillows and pillow cases to make the bed.

c. greet guest politely and confirm with the guest the extra bed or baby cot and ask for the location to set up the bed/ cot by saying " Madam/ Sir, I deliver your extra bed/ baby cot. What would be the most convenient place for you to set up the bed?"

d. make bed.

e. provide the guest with additional amenities.

III. Exercise

Translations:

1. We can bring up a fold-out bed for you.
2. Good morning, Housekeeping. May I come in?
3. The charge for the extra bed is RMB300 yuan per night.
4. I will vacuum your room right away and make your bed later.
5. I'm sorry to disturb you, but may I make up the room now?
6. 我去重新拿个吹风机给您。
7. 我可以挪动您桌上的物品吗？以便我掸灰尘。
8. 事实上，夜床服务通常不会花很长时间。我们会应客人要求提前做好。
9. 您需要我什么时候回来给您打扫房间呢？
10. 有些酒店会在客人枕头上放一小块巧克力，以此祝愿客人做个"甜蜜的梦"。

Choose the names of items that match the pictures, and write them down under the pictures.

1st line: hairdryer, rubbish bin, slippers, toilet roll

2nd line: drink packets, toiletries, safe, bedside lamp

3rd line: bathrobe, towel, pillow &quilt, cups

Reading:

1. F   2. T   3. T   4. F   5. F

Scene Two — Laundry Service

I. Activities

1. Express Service

Dialogue-Scripts:

Scene: A guest calls for laundry service, and the receptionist recommends the express service.

(R=Receptionist, G=Guest)

R: Hello, reception. How can I help you?

G: Hello. This is Mr. Jason in room 1225. I need to get my suit cleaned right away. I have an important meeting this evening. Do you have a dry cleaning service?

R: Yes. But we usually pick up laundry before 9:00 a.m. Now it's 10:00. I'm afraid your laundry can't be returned today.

G: But I have to wear it today.

R: Don't worry. We have an express service.

G: How much do you charge for the express service?

R: We charge 80 RMB for your suit. There is an extra charge of 50% for the express service.

G: That's fine. Do I need to pay for that now?

R: No, we can add it to your room account.

G: When can it be returned?

R: In three hours.

G: Great. The suit is in my car. Can you send someone to pick it up?

R: Sure, sir. I will send the bellman to pick up the car key from your room now.

G: Thank you very much.

R: You're welcome.

Answers:

Guest's Name: Mr. Jason
Room Number: 1225
Items to Be Cleaned: A suit
Method of Cleaning: Dry cleaning, express service
Charge : 80 RMB
Payment: Adding it to the room account
Time The Laundry Will Be Returned: In three hours

Practice:

1. If you have any laundry, please leave it in the laundry bag behind the bathroom door.
2. The laundry man comes over to collect it every morning.
3. Please tell us or notify in the laundry list whether you need your clothes ironed, washed, dry-cleaned or mended and also what time you want to get them back.
4. Usually, it takes about two days to have laundry done.
5. We charge 50% more for express service, but it only takes 4 hours.

2. Special Requirements

Dialogue-Scripts:

Scene: The telephone rings. The receptionist answers the phone.

(R=Receptionist, G=Guest)

H: Good afternoon. Housekeeping. How may I help you?

G: Hello. Do you do repairs to clothes?

H: Yes, sir.

G: Good. I have some trousers that need repairing. I split them this morning, and I need to wear them tomorrow morning. Can you repair them before then?

H: Well, we can usually repair clothes within two days, but it depends on how serious the damage is, sir. Sometimes we can do it quicker. I'll send someone up in a few minutes. If they have a look at them, they'll tell you how long it will take.

G: OK. By the way, there is also a stain on my trousers. Could you clean it as well?

H: What kind of stain is it, sir?

G: I spilled some soy sauce on it.

H: We'll do our best to remove the stain. Anything else ?

G: Actually yes , my wife needs her dress washed, but I'm afraid the color will run in the wash.

H: There shouldn't be any problem, sir. We'll be very careful. But you will need to write down special instructions on your laundry list.

G: All right.

H: Is there anything else I can help you with?

G: I think that's all for now. Thank you.

H: You're welcome.

Answers:

a. The trousers are split and have a stain.

b. Not sure. It depends on how serious the damage is.

c. Soy sauce.

d. He worries that the color will run in the wash.

e. The guest should write down special instructions on the laundry list.

Practice: 略

3. Laundry Damage

Dialogue-Scripts:

Scene: A laundryman comes to the guest's room to return the dress and apologizes for the laundry damage. The guest asks for compensation.

(L= laundryman, G=Guest)

L: Laundry service. May I come in?

G: Come in, please.

L: Thank you. I've brought up the clothes you wanted us to clean. But I'm awfully sorry that there is a little laundry damage. Your silk dress was a little bit burnt due to overheating of the iron. We do apologize for this.

G: Oh, my God! Let me have a look at it. I was told your Laundry Department had wide experience in this work. How could this happen?

L: We're so sorry. It's our mistake.

G: This is a new dress. I just bought it and cost me quite a lot. Does your hotel have a policy on dealing with this kind of thing?

L: According to the hotel policies, we should pay for the damage, but the indemnity should not exceed 10 times the laundry charge. I hope you understand us.

G: What's the laundry charge?

L: 35 yuan. It's on the laundry list.

G: 35 yuan? That means I can only get 350 yuan for compensation. Are you kidding? The dress cost me 880 yuan! It's unfair.

L: I'm sorry. It's our regulation.

G: I'm not satisfied. I want to see your manager.

L: In that case, I'll get the manager to take care of the issue. Sorry to have caused you so much trouble.

Answers:

you wanted us to clean

laundry damage

overheating of the iron

wide experience

a policy on dealing with this kind of thing

10 times the laundry charge

for compensation

It's our regulation

Practice:

1. damage
2. overheating
3. policy
4. indemnity
5. compensation
6. regulation

III. Exercise

Translations:

1. Could you send someone to pick up my laundry, please?
2. I'd like this jacket dry cleaned, please.
3. Would you please fill in the laundry list?
4. It might shrink, so please wash it by hand in cold water.
5. We will do our best to remove the stain, but we can't guarantee the result.
6. 恐怕已过了今天的洗衣时间。
7. 快洗比普通洗衣要多收100%的费用。
8. 我们还有快洗服务，只需花费三个小时。
9. 洗衣袋里的衣物与洗衣单上登记的不符。
10. 您的衬衫被送错了。非常抱歉给您带来不便。

Role-play: 略

Look at the sample laundry operational flow chart below and try to describe the hotel laundry operation.

The laundry department has a basic cycle of operation with the below steps:

1. Collect Soiled Linen from beds and areas and put them on to the linen chute or on to the soiled linen carts stored on each floor pantry.
2. Transport Soiled Linen to Laundry department by trolley. Make sure that the laundry items are not dragged on the floor, this may further damage or soil the laundry.
3. Sort linen and uniforms according to their stains, size, type, color etc.
4. Wash and Dry clean the soiled linens in washers. To reduce operational cost nowadays hotels uses chemicals (bleaches, detergents, softeners etc.) while washing process to remove stains instead of treating laundry items separately before washing.
5. The washed items are dried on the dryer. The drying times and temperature vary considerable according to the type of linen / cloths.
6. Fold linen and uniforms by hand. The folded items are then stored and stacked properly according to batches.

Scene Three — Personal Service

I. Activities

1. Wake-up Service

Dialogue-Scripts:

Scene: A guest calls for a wake-up call service, and the operator answers the phone.

(O= Operator, G=Guest)

O: Good evening. Operator speaking. May I help you?

G: Good evening. This is Mr. Black in Room 1505. I was wondering if your hotel had a wake up call service.

O: Yes, sir. What kind of call would you prefer, by phone, by the computer wake-up system, or by knocking at the door?

G: By phone, please.

O: What time would you like to be woken up?

G: 6:30 a.m. I need to catch the train at 8:20.

O: OK. We will wake you up at 6:30 tomorrow morning, sir.

G: Don't forget, please.

O: Don't worry. We won't forget. Have a good sleep.

G: Thank you.

...

(6:30 next morning)

O: Good morning, Mr. Black. It's 6:30. You asked me to wake you up.

G: Oh, yes, thank you. Could you please order a cab to take me to the station?

O: Sure, sir. What time do you need the cab to be ready?

G: 7:45 will be good.

O: You will find the cab ready at the front door on time. Would you like me to send the bellman to help you with the luggage?

G: No, thanks. I can handle it. Can you please tell me how the weather is today?

O: Today is a sunny day, warm and the temperature is 25 degrees outside.

G: Nice. Thanks a lot.

O: My pleasure. Have a nice day!

Answers:

Operator speaking

in Room 1505

by phone

by knocking at the door

catch the train at 8:20

Don't worry

order a cab

at the front door

help you with the luggage

25 degrees outside

Practice: 略

2. Shoe Shining Service

Dialogue-Scripts:

Scene: A guest calls for shoe-shining service, and the operator answers the phone.

(O= Operator, G=Guest)

O: Good morning. Operator speaking. How can I help you?

G: Good morning. I need to have my shoes polished. Do you have a shoe-shining service?

O: Yes. There is a shoe-shiner in the wardrobe. We also have a shoe-shining machine. If you like, I'll send someone up to take your shoes to the shoe polishing room.

G: Great! I'd like to try the shoe-shining machine. When can I get my shoes back?

O: In about 20 minutes.

G: That would be fine. By the way, is it complimentary or do I need to pay for it?

O: It's complimentary. Sir, may I have your name and room number, please?

G: Oh, this is Ralph in Room1507.

O: OK. The room attendant will come in five minutes. Is there anything else I can do for you?

G: Yes. Could you get some more drinks in the mini-bar of my room? I need five tins of Coca-Cola and some mineral water.

O: OK. The room attendant will be up in a minute.

G: Thank you very much.

O: You are welcome.

Answers:

a. The hotel offers a shoe-shiner in the wardrobe and a shoe-shining machine.

b. In the wardrobe.

c. About 20 minutes.

d. It's free.

e. Five tins of Coca-Cola and some mineral water.

Practice:

We have a shoe-shining service in our hotel. There's shoe- shining equipment in the wardrobe. We also have a shoe-shining machine. If you like, I'll send someone up to take your shoes to the shoe polishing room. Your shoes will be returned in about 20 minutes.

3. Baby-sitting Service

Dialogue-Scripts:

Scene: A guest who wants to use a baby-sitting service is talking to the room attendant.

(A=Attendant, G=Guest)

G: Would you do me a favor?

A: Certainly, if I can do it.

G: My husband and I are going out for dinner tonight. Could you look after my children till we come back?

A: I see. But I'm afraid that's impossible. It's against our hotel regulations for me to provide this service.

G: What should I do then?

A: Don't worry, madam. Our Housekeeping Department has a very good baby-sitting service. The baby-sitters are well-trained and reliable. How old are your children?

G: My son is 8 and my daughter is 7.

A: OK, they can go to the Kid's Club or we can send a baby sitter to your room.

G: What is the Kid's Club?

A: It's a place where children can play and watch movies together.

G: That sounds fun. What time does it start?

A: It starts at 6 p.m. And finishes at 10 p.m.

G: That sounds perfect.

A: If you ask the Housekeeping, they will give you more details and send a confirmation form for you to sign.

G: All right. I'll phone them right away. Thanks for the information.

A: My pleasure.

Answers:

1. T   2. F   3. T   4. F   5. T

Practice:

b→d→a→f→c→e

4. Maintenance Service

Dialogue-Scripts:

Scene: A guest has some problems with the room facilities. She calls Room Center for help, then a maintenance man is sent to help her.

(S= Staff, G=Guest)

S: Good afternoon. Room Center. May I help you?

G: Good afternoon. I have a problem with the air-conditioner in my room and the toilet doesn't flush. Could you send someone to repair them?

S: I'm sorry to hear that. We'll send someone up to check immediately. May I have your name and room number, please?

G: It's Mrs. Shawn in Room 1822. Thank you.

S: You're welcome, Mrs. Shawn.

...

(5 minutes later)

S: (Knocking at the door) Maintenance. May I come in?

G: Come in, please.

S: Good afternoon, Mrs. Shawn. Could you tell me what the trouble is in detail?

G: My air-conditioner doesn't work. It doesn't blow any air at all.

S: Let me have a look at the remote control, please.

G: Here you are.

S: Thank you … I think the batteries should be changed. Let me replace them with new ones. Now, it's working.

G: Thanks.

S: Is there anything else I can do for you?

G: Yes, the toilet doesn't flush. I'm afraid it's clogged.

S: Don't worry. I'll take a look at it.

…

S: The toilet is all right now. You may try it.

G: Yes, it's working. Thank you very much.

S: You are welcome. If you have any problems, just call us.

G: OK. Thank you.

Answers:

a. Mrs. Shawn in Room 1822.

b. It doesn't blow any air at all.

c. He changes some batteries.

d. The toilet doesn't flush.

e. Yes, he has.

Practice: 略

III. Exercise

Translations:

1. What time would you like us to call you tomorrow morning?

2. We'll send someone to repair it immediately.

3. I need to have my shoes polished. Do you have a shoe-shining service?

4. There seems to be something wrong with the toilet in my room.

5. May I suggest you the baby-sitting service of our department?

6. 我们客房服务员明天早上6:30叫醒您。

7. 水龙头一整夜滴水。

8. 有些零件需要更换，我片刻就来。

9. 托儿中心有一些经验丰富的保姆。

10. 托儿服务每小时收费20元，最低从4小时开始计费。

Write out questions according to the answers.

1. What time would you like to be woken up?

2. Could you tell me what the trouble is in detail?
3. How long shall I wait ?
4. Do you offer a baby-sitting service in the hotel?
5. May I have your name and room number, please?
6. Is it complimentary or do I need to pay for it?

Writing: 略

Part 3　Food & Beverage Department　餐饮服务英语

Brainstorm Answers:

staff:　host, hostess, waiter, waitress, captain, supervisor, assistant manager, manager, storekeeper, chef, cook, busboy, wine steward, bartender, server, kitchen helper

services:　food and beverage, room service, bar service, etc.

Scene One　Welcoming Guests

I. Activities

1. Serving Reserved Guests

Dialogue-Scripts:

(H=Host, G=Guest)

Dialogue A:

H: Good evening, madam. Welcome to our restaurant.

G: Good evening.

H: Do you have a reservation, madam?

G: Yes. My name is Sophia. I've reserved a table for two this evening.

H: Please wait for a minute. Yes, here it is, 5:00 p.m., Summer Hall. It's on the first floor. Please follow me.

G: Thank you.

Dialogue B:

H: Good evening, Mr Black. Welcome to Golden Palace. How are you doing today?

G: Everything is fine. Thank you. I've made a reservation this morning under my name. I want the same private room as last time. We have eight people this time.

H: No problem, Mr Black … you come a little bit early this time, the private room will be ready at 6:30 p.m., as you reserved. And the Rose Hall is on the second floor. I will show you up.

G: That's great! Thank you.

H: We were expecting you, Mr Black. This way, please.

Dialogue C:

H: Good evening, sir and madam. Welcome to Golden Palace. Do you have a reservation?

G: Yes, we do. A reservation for ten, in the name of Sean Steven.

H: Just a moment, please … Here it is, 7:30 p.m., a party of ten, Tulip Hall on the third floor.

G: Thank you.

H: We were expecting you, Mr Steven. This way, please.

Answers:

Golden Palace Restaurant		Table Reservation		
	Guest's Name	No. of People	Time	Private Room
1st Guest	Sophia	Two	5:00 p.m.	Summer Hall
2nd Guest	Mr Black	Eight	6:30 p.m.	Rose Hall
3rd Guest	Sean Steven	Ten	7:30 p.m.	Tulip Hall

Practice:

1. Welcome the guests.
2. Ask whether there is a reservation.
3. If there is a reservation, confirm the reservation with guests and direct them to the table.

2. Serving Non-reserved Guests

Dialogue-Scripts:

(H=Host, G=Guest)

Dialogue A:

H: Good evening, sir. Welcome to Silver Cloud Restaurant. How many people, please?

G: A table for nine, please.

H: Certainly, sir. Have you made a reservation, sir?

G: No, I'm afraid not.

H: I'm sorry, we don't have a table for nine right now, but there will be one after 15 minutes, do you mind waiting in the lounge? You can read magazines or have a drink there.

G: Ok.

H: May I have your name, please?

G: James.

H: Thank you, Mr James. We will seat you when we have a table.

Dialogue B:

H: Good afternoon, madam.

G: Good afternoon. Do you have a table for four?

H: Yes, madam. Do you have a reservation?

G: No.

H: That's fine. How about the table near that window?

G: That would be nice! Thanks.

H: Great. Come with me, please.

Answers:

Dialogue A:

a. F   b. T   c. T   d. F

Dialogue B:

a. F   b. F   c. T   d. T

Practice:

1. Do you have a reservation?
2. Did you make a reservation?
3. Did you reserve a table?
4. Have you made a reservation?

3. Changing the Table

Dialogue-Scripts:

(H=Host, G=Guest)

H: Good evening, sir and madam. How many people, please?

G: Two. And I made a reservation online yesterday. I reserved a table for two near the window under the name of Thomas.

H: Please wait for a minute, sir. Let me check it for you … yes, Mr. Thomas, a table for two. Please follow me.

G: Thank you.

H: Here it is.

G: Oh, it looks pretty narrow here in the corner. I don't think it's suitable for us. Can we change a table?

H: Well, if you don't like this one, where would you like to sit, sir?

G: Can we change our table to this one? It's much more spacious here.

H: I'm sorry, sir. The window tables have all been taken. How about the table over there? It's further back but spacious. And you can still enjoy the view of the lake.

G: Ok. That's fine.

H: This way, please. Here is your table, sir and madam.

G: Thank you. It's much better here and it makes us more relax. We can still enjoy the view of the lake though it's a little bit further from the window. That's ok.

H: I'm so glad you like it. Please wait for a minute, the waiter will be with you right away.

G: Thank you.

Answers:

made a reservation online, a table for two, check it for you, in the corner, change a table, have all been taken, Here is your table, enjoy the view of the lake, will be with you

Practice:

1. Being not satisfied with the location, environment, etc.
2. Coming late without reservation.

3. Coming when restaurant is full.

4. For special reasons like emergency, guests' favorites, etc.

III. Exercise

Translations:

1. Please wait for a minute … yes, here it is, 7:00 p.m., No. 608 private room.

2. Your table will be ready at 6:00 p.m., as you reserved.

3. How about the table over there? It's further back but spacious.

4. Well, if you don't like this one, where would you like to sit, sir?

5. Please wait for a minute, the waiter will be with you right away.

6. 欢迎来到我们餐厅。请问您有预约吗?

7. 我们正恭候您呢,赖斯夫人（Mrs Rice）,请这边走。

8. 很抱歉,我们现在没有九个人的桌子。

9. 20分钟之后会有一个餐位,您介意在大厅里等一下吗?我们有了座位就联系您。

10. 很抱歉,先生。靠窗的座位都有人了。

Role-play: 略

Answers to the questions:

a. Keep note of how many people are in a party and what table they are at. Also keep note of who is still there .

b. We can say "I will be right with you," make eye contact, or a simple hand gesture.

c. Greet them with a smile and welcome them to the restaurant by saying "Welcome to our restaurant" .

d. If there is a wait, make sure to get everyone's name right away. Explain that we currently have a short wait, and that there should be a table ready momentarily, or we are currently getting tables cleared and set.

Scene Two — Taking Orders

I. Activities

1. Western Food

Dialogue-Scripts:

(W=Waiter, G=Guest)

W: Good evening, sir. Take your seat, please.

G: Thank you.

W: Here is the menu. I will be right back to take your order. Please take your time.

G: Ok.

(a few minutes later …)

W: Excuse me, sir. May I take your order, now?

G: Yes, please. I'd like a chicken salad for the starter, a French onion soup, and a beef steak for the main course.

W: How do you like your steak, sir? Rare, medium or well done?

G: Rare, please.

W: And do you want French fries or a baked potato with the steak?

G: I'd like some French fires, and some mushroom sauce, please.

W: And for your dessert?

G: I'd like a chocolate ice cream.

W: Sure, sir. Would you like something to drink with your meal?

G: Yes. A glass of draft beer, please.

W: All right, sir. You ordered a chicken salad, a French onion soup, a rare beef steak with French fries and mushroom sauce, a chocolate ice cream and a glass of draft beer. Is that all?

G: Yes, I think it's enough.

W: Thank you, sir. Your dish will be ready soon.

Answers:

a. Here is the menu. I will be right back to take your order. Please take your time.

b. He orders a chicken salad, a French onion soup, and a beef steak.

c. He'd like a rare steak with some French fires and some mushroom sauce.

d. A chocolate ice cream and a glass of draft beer.

e. Thank you, sir. Your dish will be ready soon.

Practice:

1. Starter / Appetizer
2. Soup
3. Entree / Main Course
4. Dessert
5. Beverage

2. Chinese Food

Dialogue-Scripts:

(W=Waiter, G1= Mr James, G2=Mrs James)

W: Good afternoon, sir and madam. Would anyone like a drink to start with?

G1: Yes, Jasmine Tea, please. Let me have a look at the menu, first.

W: Certainly, sir. Here is our menu, please take your time.

(two minutes later …)

W: Excuse me, sir and madam. May I take your order, now?

G1: Almost. I don't know much about Chinese food. We would like something delicious in typical Chinese style. But I have no idea about Chinese food.

W: I see. Chinese food is divided into eight big cuisines, or say, eight styles, such as Cantonese food, Beijing food, Sichuan food, etc. Most Sichuan dishes are spicy and hot. And they taste differently. Which kind of food do you prefer, light, heavy, sweet or spicy?

G2: We are not used to oily and spicy food.

W: How about steamed pork ribs with rice powder? It's very tasty and it's our chef's specialty today.

G1: Sounds great. Is it large or small?

W: We have two choices. Small has 4 pieces and large has 8 pieces.

G1: So we'd like a small one.

G2: Would you tell me how the "steamed prawn with garlic sauce" is cooked? It looks so delicious.

W: Well, it's a very popular local seafood. The fresh prawns are steamed with garlic, soy sauce, white pepper, sesame oil and Chinese wine.

G2: I'd like to have this, please.

W: Certainly, madam.

G1: And a lettuce with oyster sauce, please.

W: Sure. Do you like soup? We have ham and white gourd soup, tomato and egg soup, seaweed egg soup, and so on.

G2: Tomato and egg soup.

W: Ok, tomato and egg soup. And what would you like to go with your dishes, fried rice, noodles, or steamed bread?

G1: Fried rice, please.

W: Anything else?

G1: I think that's it for now.

W: Certainly, sir. You ordered a steamed pork ribs with rice powder, a steamed prawn with garlic sauce, a lettuce with oyster sauce, a tomato and egg soup, and rice. The dishes will come out in about 15 minutes.

G1: Thank you

Answers:

a. T   b. F   c. F   d. F   e. T   f. T

Practice:

1. Sweet and Sour Mandarin Fish (Jiangsu Cuisine) 松鼠桂鱼
2. Hotpot (Sichuan Cuisine) 火锅
3. Stewed Turtle with Ham (Anhui Cuisine) 火腿炖甲鱼
4. Four Joy Meatballs (Shandong Cuisine) 四喜丸子
5. Dongpo Pork (Zhejiang Cuisine) 东坡肉
6. Spicy Chicken (Hunan Cuisine) 辣子鸡
7. Dry-Fried Beef and Noodles (Guangdong Cuisine) 干炒牛河
8. Buddha Jumping Wall (Fujian Cuisine) 佛跳墙

3. Buffet

Dialogue-Scripts:

(W=Waiter, G=Guest)

W: Good evening, sir and madam. How many people, please?

G: Well, we have six people today. Do you have buffet in your restaurant?

W: Yes, sir. We have a buffet. You can have all you want for 138 yuan.

G: Do you have seafood for buffet?

W: Yes. We have a good selection of seafood, meat, dim sum and vegetables.

G: What drinks do you have?

W: We serve various kinds of soft drinks, such as milk, coffee, juice, lemonade and coke. We also serve several simple wines, like beer or red wine.

G: Great. We would like to have buffet here.

W: Certainly, sir. Would you like to sit here by the window?

G: Perfect. Thank you.

W: By the way, tableware and dishes are on the main buffet table over there, and the drinks are by the wall. Please help yourself.

G: Thank you!

Answers:

we have six people today, 138 yuan, seafood, meat, dim sum, vegetables, milk, coffee, juice, lemonade, coke, tableware, dishes.

Practice:

Advantages:

1. It is a fast service.
2. It requires less staff to render the service needed.
3. The presentation of the different dishes can be appetizing.

Disadvantages:

It may result in shortage of food especially when the early ones may serve themselves more; thus very little food is left for the latecomers.

III. Exercise

Translations:

1. Here is the menu. I will be right back to take your order.
2. And do you want French fries or spaghetti with the steak?
3. Which dishes do you prefer, light, heavy, sweet or spicy?
4. We have a good selection of seafood, meat, dim sum and vegetables.
5. Tableware and dishes are on the main buffet table over there. Please help yourself.
6. 您要点些喝的吗?

7. 我们想要品尝一些中国特色的美味菜肴。
8. 我们有火腿冬瓜汤，番茄蛋汤，紫菜蛋汤等。
9. 您想要什么主食搭配菜肴，炒饭，面条还是饺子？
10. 是的，先生。我们有自助餐。您付138元，就可以品尝所有的菜。

Role-play: 略

Discussion:

a. F　　b. T　　c. F　　d. T　　e. T　　f. F

Scene Three — Serving Dishes

I. Activities

1. Slow in Serving

Dialogue-Scripts:

(W=Waiter, G=Guest)

W: Yes, madam?

G: We ordered the lunch meal as soon as we arrived. There are at least twenty minutes past and our lunch still hasn't come yet. Why is it taking so long?

W: I'm very sorry, madam. I will check your order with the chef right now.

G: Please, we have to attend a very important meeting this afternoon in 30 minutes!

W: I understand, madam. Just a moment, please.

　　(three minutes later …)

W: Sorry to have kept you waiting, madam. Here is your meal. We are very sorry for the delay. Here are two sodas for you. They are free of charge. Please enjoy your lunch.

G: That's ok. Thank you.

Answers:

a. twenty　　　　　　b. the chef　　　　　　c. thirty

d. "We are very sorry for the delay"

e. two soda completely free

Practice:

a. The waiters need to get familiar with the items on the menu to improve the efficiency.

b. Improve the serving skills of the waiters.

c. Confirm orders with guests and keep checking the orders with chefs as much as possible.

d. To make sure the restaurant has enough waiters, chefs and stoves.

2. Serving Wrong Dish

Dialogue-Scripts:

(W=Waiter, G=Guest)

Dialogue A:

G: Excuse me, waiter.

W: Yes, sir. What can I do for you?

G: I'm afraid we haven't order this dish. I think there must be something wrong.

W: I'm very sorry, sir. What was your order?

G: We ordered two shrimp noodles, not this fried rice.

W: I'm sorry for that, sir. May I take it away, please? Thank you. I'd like to check the order soon.

G: Ok.

W: We are very sorry to have caused you this trouble.

Dialogue B:

W: Is there anything I can do for you?

G: Yes. We ordered a spiced spring chicken in chili, but you served us the steamed chicken with rice flour.

W: I'm awfully sorry, sir. There must have been some mistake. I do apologize for giving you the wrong dish. I'll check the order with the chef and bring your dish soon.

G: Hope it won't take so long.

(3 minutes later …)

W: Excuse me, sir. Your dish will be ready in about 15 minutes. I'm so sorry about it. If you don't mind, please try this steamed chicken with rice flour. I will cross it off your bill. And here is the complementary drink for you while waiting. They are all on the house.

G: Well, that's fine. Thanks.

W: I'm very sorry for the mistake. I assure you it won't happen again. Please take your time and enjoy yourself.

Answers:

Dialogue A:

a. F   b. F   c. F   d. T

Dialogue B:

a. T   b. F   c. T   d. F

Practice:

- Be genuine: Show concern and understanding of their feelings.
- Be brief: Don't make excuses. The customer does not want to know whose fault it is, they just want it fixed.
- Give a time for correcting the situation: "Now" "shortly" "as soon as possible".

3. Special Service

Dialogue-Scripts:

(W=Waiter, G=Guest)
The waiter is serving dishes for a family of four.

W: Excuse me, sir. May I serve your dishes now?

G: Yes, please.

W: Here are your dishes. This one is tomato fish pieces, and this one is grilled pigeon.

G: They smell so good. Thank you.

W: You are welcome, sir. Does the high chair work well for your little son?

G: Yes, it's just suitable for him. Thank you.

W: Great, if you need any help, please let me know.

G: Sure, thanks!

    (two minutes later ...)

W: Excuse me, sir. Here is your noodle. It's very hot, please take care.

G: Thank you.

W: How do you like the food?

G: Well, it's very delicious and fresh.

W: I'm so happy to hear that. By the way, here is the flatware for your daughter, 3-piece child set. They are smaller, easier and safer for your child to cut and eat the food. And this little toy car is for your baby son.

G: Wow, that's very kind of you. Thank you so much, they are so happy to have the dinner here!

W: It's my pleasure. Shall I change this plate to a smaller one?

G: Sure, go ahead.

W: Thank you, sir. Do you need anything else?

G: No, everything is perfect. Thank you!

W: You are welcome, sir. Wish you have a good time with your family!

Answers:

May I serve your dishes now, work well for your little son, Here is your noodle, delicious and fresh, 3-piece child set, little toy car, a smaller one, Do you need anything else

Practice:

a vegetarian guest — a meal without meat

a guest with a baby — high chair

a guest with gluten allergies — gluten-free food

a guest who is on diet — healthy foods that are low in fat and calories

a guest who wants to save time — fast food

a Muslim guest — Muslim food

III. Exercise

Translations:

1. Here are two sodas for you. They are free of charge. Please enjoy your lunch.
2. I do apologize for giving you the wrong dish. I'll check the order with the chef and bring your dish soon.
3. Sorry to have kept you waiting. Your dish will be ready in about 15 minutes.
4. I'm very sorry for the mistake. I assure you it won't happen again.
5. Here is the flatware for your daughter, 3-piece child set. Wish you have a good time with your family!
6. 很抱歉，先生，一定是出了什么问题。
7. 太好了，如果您需要任何帮助，请告诉我。
8. 如果您不介意，请您品尝一下这道菜。我会在账单上把这道菜划掉。
9. 这是在您等菜的时候为您提供的免费饮料。
10. 我可以把这个盘子换成小一点的吗？

Role-play:略

Reading :

a. F   b. T   c. F   d. F

Scene Four — Bar Services

I. Activities

1. Serving Wines

Dialogue-Scripts:

(B=Bartender, G1=Guest 1, G2=Guest 2)

B: Good evening, sir. Welcome to our bar. What can I do for you?

G1: Yes, could you recommend something to drink?

B: Certainly, sir. We serve brandy, whiskey, gin, vodka and so on. What would you like?

G1: I'd like a Scottish gin.

B: With soda or water?

G1: No. Just a double Scottish gin on the rocks, please.

B: Yes, sir. What would you like, sir?

G2: I think I'll just have a beer. What kind of beer do you have here?

B: We have bottled beer, stout and draught beer.

G2: Ok, just bring me a tall glass of draught beer.

B: Certainly, sir. Please wait for a moment. I will be right back with your drinks.

(Several minutes later ...)

B: Here are your drinks, a double Scottish gin on the rocks and a glass of draught beer.

G1 and G2: Thank you.

B: Would you like anything else? How about snacks, such as potato chips or pretzels?

G1: No, thanks. By the way, do you take credit cards here or shall I pay in cash?

B: Well, you may sign the bill since you are staying at our hotel, the hotel will charge you when you leave.

G1: I see. Thank you.

B: My pleasure. Enjoy your drink!

Answers:

a. T   b. F   c. F   d. F   e. F

Practice:

a. onion rings,   b. fried peanuts   c. potato chips

d. pretzel   e. pop corn   f. chicken wings

2. Communicating with Guests

Dialogue-Scripts:

(B=Bartender, G=Guest)

B: Good evening. Did you enjoy your drink, sir?

G: Yes, it was great! You know, I enjoy the music and the cocktail here very much.

B: I'm so glad you like it. Would you like to try another kind of our new style? It's called Lychee Martini and it's also very popular.

G: What is it like?

B: Well, it's a special cocktail mixed with vodka, lychee juice and vermouth.

G: Sounds great. But I'm fine with the beer tonight. Maybe next time.

B: Certainly, sir.

G: How long have you been working here?

B: About two years. I enjoy working here because I can meet different people and make friends with them. So where are you from?

G: I'm from Seattle, United States. And this is my first time in Nanjing.

B: Do you like the city?

G: Yes, I think it's a very beautiful city and rich in culture. I traveled a lot but I really enjoy staying here.

B: You are right. It is the capital city of six or ten dynasties in ancient Chinese history, it has a brilliant cultural heritage, like the Purple Mountain, Dr. Sun Yat-sen's Mausoleum, and so on. Are you here on vacation or business?

G: On vacation.

B: If you have time, I should say that one of the must-see places in the city would be the area around the Qinhuai River. You can also visit Confucius Temple there to go shopping and buy several souvenirs.

G: Sounds so interesting. I will definitely try. Thank you for your information. You are so kind.

B: My pleasure, sir. Have a nice evening!

Answers:

a. Yes. He enjoys the music and the cocktail there very much.

b. It's called Lychee Martini.

c. About two years.

d. He is from Seattle, United States. And this is his first time in Nanjing.

e. "So where are you from?" "Do you like the city?" "Are you here on vocation or business?"

Practice:

hobbies, hometown, experiences in the city, jobs, favorite drinks, sports, attractions in the city, etc.

3. Conflict Resolution

Dialogue-Scripts:

(B=Bartender, G=Guest)

B: Good evening, sir. How many people, please?

G: Well, we have five people today.

B: Would you like a table for five?

G: Yes.

B: Follow me, please. Will this table do?

G: It's fine. Do you have any imported beers?

B: Yes. We have Heineken, Budweiser and Carlsberg. Which would you like?

G: Please give us five bottles of Heineken.

B: Certainly, sir. Anything else?

G: No, thanks.

(About an hour later, two of the guests get drunk. One of them begins to shout and the other one begins to sing loudly …)

B: Excuse me, sir. Is everything all right? Do you need some tea or water now? I think your friends may need it.

G: Sorry to disturb other guests here. Yes, some tea will be great.

B: I will come with the tea right now. Maybe your friends will feel better when they have more fresh air, sir. It's very stuffy and noisy here.

G: Yeah, I understand. Sorry.

Answers:

we have five people today, any imported beers, five bottles of Heineken, Is everything all right, some tea will be great, they have more fresh air

Practice:

1. Drunks respond better to someone who approaches them in a friendly manner rather than an authoritative manner.
2. Whenever possible, involve the drunk's sober friend or colleague.
3. Drunks do not like to be told what to do.
4. A drunk can sense your fear — so be confident yet non-threatening with them and show genuine concern for their well being.
5. Ask them questions about themselves.

III. Exercise

Translations:

1. You may sign the bill since you are staying at our hotel, the hotel will charge you when you leave.
2. We serve brandy, whiskey, gin, vodka and so on. What would you like?
3. Would you like anything else? How about snacks, such as potato chips or pretzels?
4. Are you here on vocation or business?
5. Your friends will feel better when they have more fresh air, sir. It's very stuffy and noisy here.
6. 您现在需要一些茶或者水吗？我想您的朋友可能需要。
7. 您愿意尝试一下我们另一种新品吗？
8. 我喜欢在这里工作，因为可以见到不同的人，并和他们成为朋友。
9. 您在这里工作多久了？
10. 打扰了，先生。这里一切都好吗？

Role-play: 略

Reading:

a. T   b. F   c. T   d. F   e. T   f. T

Scene Five Room Services

I. Activities

1. Doorknob Menu

Dialogue-Scripts:

(R=Receptionist, G=Guest)

R: Good evening, reception. May I help you?

G: Good evening. This is Susan Jones from Room 4399. I'd like to have breakfast in my room tomorrow morning.

R: Certainly, Ms Jones. You can simply press "0" or Service Express on your telephone for all of your room service needs. Or you can use our Breakfast Door Knob Menu. The menu offers many dining choices from breakfast selections, sandwiches, burgers, entrees to pizza served in your room. It is a convenient way to order your breakfast in advance. Just put it out on your doorknob before you go to sleep. Your breakfast will be delivered to your room at your requested time.

G: Sounds great. What time do you usually serve breakfast in the morning?

R: Breakfast can be served in your room from 7:00 a.m. until 10:00 a.m.

G: I see. Thank you for your information. I will read Door Knob Menu right now.

R: You are welcome. Have a nice evening!

Answers:

a. Susan Jones from Room 4399.

b. Press "0" or Service Express on your telephone, or use the Breakfast Door Knob Menu.

c. The menu offers many dining choices from breakfast selections, sandwiches, burgers, entrees to pizza.

d. Choose the food on the menu and put it out on the doorknob before go to sleep. The breakfast will be delivered to the room at the guest's requested time.

e. Breakfast can be served from 7:00 a.m. until 10:00 a.m.

Practice:

Door knob breakfast menu order collection:

1. The overnight Supervisor shall assign a waiter to collect all door knob breakfast menu orders every night floor by floor.
2. Write down the room number on each door knob breakfast menu order.
3. Preparing the bill for the breakfast service.
4. Sort out all the prepared bills according to the time of service, starting from the earliest one, with priority given to the VIP rooms.

2. Ordering Meals

Dialogue-Scripts:

(W=Waiter, G=Guest)

W: Hello, room service. Can I help you?

G: We'd like to order some food, please.

W: Certainly, sir. What would you like?

G: Is everything on the menu?

W: Yes, everything is on the menu.

G: I'd like a Caesar salad, a tuna sandwich and a Penne Pasta.

W: Would you like anything to drink?

G: Yes, a glass of grapefruit juice and a cup of coffee, please.

W: What kind of coffee would you prefer, caramel macchiato or vanilla latte?

G: Vanilla latte, please.

W: A Caesar salad, a tuna sandwich, a Penne Pasta, a glass of grapefruit juice and a cup of vanilla latte. Is that right?

G: Yes, that's right. How long will it take?

W: Your lunch will be ready in about 15 minutes.

G: Perfect. We are really hungry now. By the way, is there an extra charge for the room service?

W: Yes, we add a 10 percent service charge. May I know your name and your room number, please?

G: Peter Chen in room 1508.

W: Thank you for calling, Mr Chen. Your meal will be prepared soon.

Answers:

ROOM SERVICE RECORD	NO. OF PEOPLE: TWO
TIME: 11:40 A.M.	
FOOD	a Caesar salad, a tuna sandwich, a Penne Pasta
DRINK	a glass of grapefruit juice, a cup of coffee
GUEST'S NAME	Peter Chen
ROOM NUMBER	1508

Practice:

a. Greet the guest.

b. Ask the guest's need: food, drinks, special needs.

c. Answer the questions or give the suggestions to the guest if necessary.

d. Ask the guest's name and the room number.

e. Confirm the order again.

f. Tell the guest the order will be ready very soon.

3. Serving Meals

Dialogue-Scripts:

(W=Waiter, G=Guest)

W: Room service. May I come in?
G: Come in, please.
W: Good evening, Mr Bacon . Here is the dinner you ordered.
G: Thank you, just put it on the table, please.
W: Certainly, sir. Here is your mixed green salad, a smoked salmon and a bottle of beer. Shall I pour you a glass of beer straight away, Mr Bacon?
G: No, thanks. I'll pour it myself in a minute.
W: Ok. Here is your bill. Would you please sign your name here?
G: No problem. Here you are.
W: Thank you, Mr Bacon. We will add the cost to your room bill. If you need anything else, please feel free to call us. We are always at your service.
G: Thank you.
W: You are welcome. Have a pleasant evening!

Answers:

Room service, just put it on the table, mixed green salad, a smoked salmon, a bottle of beer, Here you are, please feel free to call us

Practice:

a. glassware b. lines and napkins c. in-room dinning menu
d. flatware e. dishwater f. room service cart

III. Exercise

Translations:

1. Breakfast can be served in your room from 7:00 a.m. until 10:00 a.m.
2. You can simply press "0" or Service Express on your telephone for all of your room service needs.
3. The menu offers many dining choices from breakfast selections, sandwiches, burgers, entrees to pizza served in your room.
4. Room service. May I come in?
5. If you need anything else, please feel free to call us.
6. 您想要哪种咖啡，焦糖玛奇朵还是香草拿铁？
7. 您点的菜马上就准备好。
8. 您可以使用我们的早餐门把菜单。这种提前预订早餐的方式非常方便。
9. 在您睡觉前把它放在您的门把手上即可。
10. Bacon先生，我需要直接给您倒一杯啤酒吗？

Role-play: 略

Reading:

a. Once the order is delivered to the room, the room service server will go over the order with the hotel guest to be sure it is correct.
b. When guests are done with their food trays, the server is responsible for picking up the dirty dishes and bringing them back to the kitchen.
c. Yes, he will.
d. The people who have customer service skills or have had a job serving customers within the food industry. Moreover, servers should also be neat in appearance and have a pleasant attitude with the customers and the other hotel employees.

Part 4　Other Services　其他服务英语

Brainstorm Answers:

people:　coach, masseur, masseuse ...
places:　indoor swimming pool, fitness center, bowling room, tennis court ...
things:　recreation facility, recreational sports apparatus, weight equipment, bar bell, chest expander, stationary bike, shower, fitness, wellness ...
services: sauna, massage, reduce tension, relax ...

Scene One　Conference Service

I. Activities

1. Introduction of Facilities

Dialogue-Scripts:

Scene: The Convention Service Manager, Mike is introducing meeting facilities to a guest who wants to hold a conference in the hotel.

(M=Manager, C=Customer)

M: I'm the Convention Service Manager. My name is Mary. What can I do for you?

C: We want to hold a conference in your hotel.

M: When will the conference be?

C: From October 25th to 29th.

M: What kind of conference will you hold and how many people will attend, Mr. Washington?

C: It's an International Academic Seminar. The exact number of delegates has not been finalized. We expect that 300 participants will attend the conference.

M: We have two large conference halls. One seats 400 people; the other can accommodate up to 600 attendees.

C: Do you have any small meeting rooms and small exhibition rooms?

M: Yes, we have 8 small meeting rooms which can hold 40 to 60 people and a small exhibition room.

C: Good. I'd like to book a large conference hall for 3 days and 6 small meeting rooms for two days.

M: OK. What meeting facilities do you need?

C: We need a multi-media projector, and a video-camera in the large room as well as a multi-media projector and a flip chart in each small room.

M: No problem. Anything else?

C: I also need an English interpreter and two messengers.

M: OK. Everything will be ready then.

C: Thank you. I need to consult with the organizer. I'll let you know by email once we've decided.

M: OK. Mr. Washington, may I have your contact number please?

C: My telephone number is 15051964337.

M: Thank you. We look forward to your reply.

Answers:

Conference Date: From October 25th to 29th
Conference Name: International Academic Seminar
Number of Participants: 300 participants
Conference Hall Booked: A large conference hall and 6 small meeting rooms
Meeting Facilities: A multi-media projector, and a video-camera in the large room and a multi-media projector, flip chart in each small room
Other requirements: An English interpreter and two messengers
Contact Number of The Guest: 15051964337

Practice:

We need to know how many attendees, what kind of the meeting, the time, the organizer, special requirements for the meeting, the customs or habits of attendees, how to pay, etc.

2. Contract Negotiation

Dialogue-Scripts:

Scene: Martin Washington comes to the hotel to discuss the terms with Susan, the convention service manager.

(M=Manager, C=Customer)

M: Pleased to meet you, Mr. Washington. I'm Susan. I've been expecting you.

C: Pleased to meet you, too, Susan. I'd like to discuss some details of the conference service with you.

M: Have you finalized the number of participants?

C: Yes, we have 350 attendees in all. I want to make some changes to what I told you about the conference halls last time. We'll need the large conference hall from October 25th to 27th, and 8 small meeting rooms from October 28th to 29th. The facilities are the same.

M: OK. Would you like some rooms?

C: Yes, we'd like to reserve 160 standard rooms. And 30 deluxe rooms for the V.I.Ps in all.

M: Could you show me a guest list so that I can assign the proper rooms for them?

C: Here you are. Is there any discount for conference reservation?

M: Yes. I went to see the General Manager yesterday, and he agreed to give you 10% off for the whole package.

C: Thank you very much.

M: It's my pleasure. Could you tell me your catering requirements for the conference?

C: The suppers on the first day and the last day of the conference are banquets with some wine. The other meals are buffets.

M: OK. We have Burgundy and some famous Chinese wine, like Great Wall, Dynasty and Chateau Changyu-Castel. They taste good and the price is reasonable.

C: Well, please provide some Burgundy and Great Wall for the banquet.

M: OK. I'll make the arrangement. Would you follow me to my office to sign the printed contract please?

C: Yeah. Thanks for your help.

Answers:

discuss some details

finalized the number of participants

October 25th to 27th

160 standard rooms

30 deluxe rooms

a guest list

give you 10% off

catering requirements

banquets with some wine

the price is reasonable

sign the printed contract

Practice:

Etiquette and hospitality service, shuttle service, conference site arrangement, catering arrangement, secretarial service, accommodation arrangement, recreation service, tickets service, etc.

3. Conference Registration

Dialogue-Scripts:

Scene: Conference attendees come to register for the conference.

(R=Receptionist, C=Customer)

R: Good morning, madam. Would you like to register for the conference?

C: Yes.

R: Have you pre-registered?

C: Yes, I have. My name is Sophie Donald.

R: Good. Let me check it up. I've got it. Sophie Donald, from New York, am I right?

C: Yes.

R: Miss Donald, here is your meeting badge and meeting packet. The packet contains a layout of the hotel, a map of downtown Shanghai, information about scenic spots and other related items.

C: Thank you.

R: we've put you in Room 1509. It's a deluxe suite. Here is your room card.

C: Could you tell me whether my colleague Kelly Hathaway has arrived or not?

R: Yes, she has. She is in room 1510, next to yours.

C: Great! Thank you.

R: My pleasure. Amy will show you to your room, and she will serve you during the conference. Have a pleasant stay here.

Answers:

a. Yes, she has.

b. From New York.

c. Meeting badge, meeting packet and room card.

d. There is a layout of the hotel, a map of downtown Shanghai, scenic spot information and other related items.

e. Her colleague Kelly Hathaway.

Practice:

1. scenic spot   2. badge   3. layout   4. related   5. register

III. Exercise

Translations:

1. Good morning. We want to hold a meeting in your hotel. May I speak to the person in charge?
2. We have all kinds of facilities in our hotel conference hall to meet your needs.
3. How many participants will attend the meeting?
4. I'd like to have a discussion about some details of the conference service with you.
5. The suppers on the first day and the last day of the conference are banquets.
6. 他们还需要电传，影印，秘书办公服务和20台手提电脑。
7. 您能把贵宾的名单交给我们吗？以便为他们安排恰当的房间。
8. 上午好，先生。请问您是开会报到吗？
9. Robinson先生，您的房间号是2312。这是一个豪华套间。给您房卡，这是您的会议证章和会议袋。
10. 来自哥伦比亚大学的Moran博士前来开会报到，他预先登记过。

Role-play: 略

The following is a list of conference facilities. Please find the items that match Chinese phrases in the table below.

电影放映机　　（ K ）　　　　笔记本电脑　　（ G ）
耳机　　　　　（ A ）　　　　麦克风　　　　（ B ）
视听设备　　　（ H ）　　　　扩音器　　　　（ C ）
幻灯片投影仪　（ I ）　　　　活动挂图　　　（ D ）
电视机　　　　（ L ）　　　　录像机　　　　（ M ）
白板　　　　　（ E ）　　　　多媒体投影机　（ J ）
激光打印机　　（ F ）

Scene Two　　　Recreation Services

I. Activities

1. Fitness Center

Dialogue-Scripts:

Scene: A guest goes to take exercise in the hotel gym.

(R=Receptionist, G=Guest)

R: Good afternoon, sir. Welcome to our fitness center.

G: Good afternoon. What kind of exercise can I do here?

R: Various things, like jogging, stretching, weight-lifting, and things like that. We have the latest fitness apparatus here, such as racing apparatus, exercise bicycle, spring expanders, dumb-bells and so on. You name it.

G: Sounds great! What Exercise can I do to develop my shoulder muscles?

R: You may use dumbbells. Let me show you. Sit down here and hold one dumbbell in each of your hands. Then, use your thighs to get yourself in position. Raise the dumbbells up to ear level while ensuring that your palms are facing forward. Push the dumbbells upwards and lift them up until they are fully extended on top of your head. Lower back the dumbbells down to your ear level. Then repeat this.

G: Cool. I'll have a try.

R: I think you'd better warm up first in order to avoid muscle injury.

G: Oh, I see. Thanks for your reminding me.

R: What else can I do for you?

G: Could you get a towel for me?

R: Sure, I'll be back soon. Enjoy.

Answers:

fitness center

jogging, stretching, weight-lifting

exercise bicycle

shoulder muscles

each of your hands

ear level

facing forward

extended on top of your head

warm up first

get a towel

Practice: 略

2. Beauty Salon

Dialogue-Scripts:

Scene: A hotel guest is at Beauty Salon, ready for a new hairdo. The staff member makes some suggestions to her.

(G=Guest, S=Staff)

G: I'm ready for a new hairdo. Do you have any suggestions?

S: Have you taken a look at any of the new styles lately?

G: Yes, I brought a magazine to show you. I like this one.

S: Oh, that is pretty. Do you want to keep your hair this long? Or do you want to make it shorter? I think you would look cute with short hair. Perhaps you should go even shorter than in the picture.

G: I'll leave it up to you. Like I said, I'm ready for a change.

S: OK. You should really think about getting highlights put in, too.

G: Do you think that would look good? I'm worried it will make my hair look unnatural.

S: No, it won't. The highlights are very subtle. We can do a little bit this time. If you like it, we can do more next time. Otherwise, the highlights should grow out in about four weeks.

G: OK, just do what you want. I believe in you.

　…

S: It's done. It looks wonderful!

G: Turn the chair so that I can see myself in the mirror.

S: What do you think of it?

G: Beautifully done. Many thanks.

Answers:

a. The guest brings a magazine to show the hair style she likes.

b. No, she leaves it up to the staff.

c. She is worried that it will make her hair look unnatural.

d. The highlights are very subtle.

e. Yes, she is.

Practice:

洗头（have a shampoo）　　烫发（permanent）
剪发（hair cutting）　　　打薄（thinning）
护发（hair treatment）　　染发（hair coloring）
吹风（blow）　　　　　　吹风机（hair dryer）
梳子（comb）　　　　　　发夹（hair clip）
剪刀（scissors）　　　　　发胶（gel）
定型液（hairspray）　　　头皮屑（dandruff）
发型造型师（hair designer）　美发从业人员（hairdresser）

3. Massage Center

Dialogue-Scripts:

Scene: A guest goes to the bathing center for a massage in a hotel.

(R=Receptionist, G=Guest)

R: Welcome to our bathing center, sir! Is there anything I can do for you?

G: I'd like to have a massage.

R: Are you a hotel guest?

G: Yes, I am James Ellen. My room number is 1210.

R: Thank you. We have body massage, foot massage and point massage. Which one would you like?

G: What is a point massage?

R: Point massage is a typical Chinese massage. When one point is massaged, the corresponding organ will feel better if it is hurt. Besides, Massage is helpful to relax muscles, relieve stress and improve the circulation.

G: It sounds fantastic. Does it hurt?

R: It doesn't hurt. But when the point is pressed, you might feel a bit sore. You can tell the masseuse if she is pressing too hard.

G: How much is the point massage?

R: 250 yuan per hour.

G: OK. I'd like to have a try.

S: This way, please.

Answers:

Guest's Name: James Ellen
Room Number: 1210
Massage Types in Hotel: Body massage, foot massage and point massage
Guest's Choice: Point massage
Massage Is Helpful for: Relaxing muscles, relieving stress and improving the circulation
When the point is pressed, you might feel: a bit sore
Charge for the Massage: 250 yuan per hour

Practice: 略

III. Exercise

Translations:

1. How would you like your hair cut?
2. Can you show me some patterns of hair styles?
3. I'd like to take some exercise. Could you tell me what facilities you have here?
4. You'd better do some stretches before you work out.
5. Massage is helpful to relax muscles, relieve stress and improve the circulation.
6. 我认为您留短发会很漂亮。
7. 请放松一点，闭上眼睛，平静呼吸。
8. 这项运动能让您的肩膀更有型。
9. 您可以教我怎么使用这台机器吗？
10. 您想洗发吗？

Match the terms in column A with the meanings in column B.

A-g   B-a   C-f   D-i   E-b   F-h   G-j   H-c   I-d   J-e

Describe the pictures: 略

Scene Three — Shopping Arcade

I. Activities

1. Choosing a gift

Dialogue-Scripts:

Scene: A customer is choosing some souvenirs in the shop.

(A= Assistant, C=Customer)

C: Hello. I want to buy some gifts closely related to Chinese culture as a token for my China trip.

A: You've come to the right place. We have the best souvenirs in the city.

C: Good. I need to buy a gift for my husband.

A: You could buy a seal with his name on it. We can make one for you in ten minutes.

C: Great! He will like it.

A: Could you write down his name on the paper?

C: Sure ... I also need something for myself. What do you think will be the most suitable for me?

A: Well, madam. Your shape is so gracious and slim. Would you like to have a Chinese Qipao? It's very popular in China.

C: Chipao? May I see it, please?

A: Of course. How do you like this one? It is made of pure Chinese silk. It's velvety and the color is brilliant.

C: Yeah! I like the design and the color is my favorite. Can I try it on?

A: Yes, of course. What size are you?

C: About size 13.

A: OK. The changing room is over there.

C: Thank you.

Answers:

1. F   2. F   3. T   4. F   5. F   6. T

Practice: 略

2. Chinese Porcelain

Dialogue-Scripts:

Scene: A customer is choosing some porcelain in the shop.

(A= Assistant, C=Customer)

R: What can I do for you?

C: May I have a look at that china set?

R: Yes, of course.

C: It is extremely beautiful. Where was it made?

R: It was made in Jingdezhen, the capital city of porcelain.

C: It's very nice, I'll take it.

R: OK. Is there anything else you want, madam?

C: (Pointing to a set of blue and white porcelain tableware) The porcelain tableware looks nice. May I have a look?

R: Of course. You've made a good choice, madam. This is called egg-shell china. It is known to be "as white as jade and as thin as paper". It is not for use, but for show.

C: Oh, I see. I heard it is the best quality porcelain and it is also made in Jingdezhen, isn't it?

R: Yes, you're right.

C: Oh, it must be precious. I'll take it.

R: OK. Shall I wrap them together or separately?

C: Separately, please. How much does this all cost?

R: That comes to 756 RMB.

C: OK, here's my credit card.

Answers:

china set

Where was it made

The porcelain tableware

as thin as paper

but for show

wrap them together or separately

756 RMB

credit card

Practice:

1. hometown 2. contribution 3. recognized 4. rough 5. low
6. primitive 7. from 8. experience 9. conditions 10. coated

3. Chinese Painting

Dialogue-Scripts:

Scene: A customer is choosing some Chinese paintings in the shop.

(A= Assistant, C=Customer)

R: Good afternoon. I'm especially interested in Chinese paintings. Do you have any good ones?

C: Yes, we do.

R: Wonderful. Could you tell me the difference between Western oil paintings and Chinese ink paintings?

C: Well, it's a long story. Briefly speaking, oil paintings are created by colors and brush touches while traditional Chinese paintings are by lines and strokes.

C: I see. Could you recommend some traditional Chinese paintings to me?

R: Yes, of course. We have landscape paintings, figure paintings and flower-and-bird paintings. Which one would you prefer?

C: I prefer landscape paintings.

R: Chinese landscape painting is a cultural indicator of the Chinese national spirit. How about this one?

C: So beautiful! I can almost sense peace and harmony from the painting.

R: That's true. Chinese art stresses the harmony between Man and Nature, which is an important part of China's traditional culture.

C: I love this one. How much is it?

R: RMB880 yuan.

C: I think it's too expensive. Can you come down a bit?

R: That's our rock bottom price. It cannot be lowered further.

C: OK, I'll take it.

Answers:

a. Oil paintings are created by colors and brush touches while traditional Chinese paintings are by lines and strokes.

b. There are landscape painting, figure painting and flower and-bird painting in the shop.

c. Chinese landscape painting.

d. The harmony between Man and Nature.

e. RMB880 yuan.

Practice: 略

III. Exercise

Translations:

1. I'd like to buy some real Chinese souvenirs for my friends and relatives.
2. You can look around and see if there is anything you like.
3. I can almost sense peace and harmony from those landscape paintings.
4. We have a great variety of Chinese antiques.
5. Shall I wrap them together or separately?
6. 按照中国的传统观念，仙鹤与松树都是长寿的象征。
7. 这个玉镯多少钱?看起来不错。
8. 我们所有的商品都有明确标价。
9. 我们有各种各样的礼品供您挑选。
10. 中国瓷器不仅是精美的日用品，也是珍贵的艺术品。

Discussion:

1. I should introduce the features, the relationship with Chinese culture, the perks for the customers and get ready for any other information about the souvenirs the customers want to know. Enthusiasm and patience are vital when selling our products.
2. If the discount is unavailable, we could refuse discount politely by saying something like, "I'm sorry, but the price is final". Try to emphasis the value of products and how they are worth the price.
3. Chinese knots, Chinese porcelain, Chinese seals, Chinese tea set and tea leaves, Chinese paintings and drawings, Chinese paper cuttings, Qipao(Chinese traditional dress), Chinese fan, Jade jewelry, silk scarf ...

Role-play: 略

Part 5 Emergencies & Complaints 应急和投诉处理

Brainstorm Answers:

Complain about: room reservation, room facilities, food, bad service, restaurant environment, cleanliness of tableware, wrong charge, wrong delivery …

Solution: on behalf of, apologize, terribly sorry, inconvenience, look into the matter, take a note, handle, assure, discount …

Scene One Handling Emergency

I. Activities

1. Asking for a Doctor

DialogueA-Scripts:

Scene: A guest gets hurt in the room. Her husband is calling the front desk for help.

(R=Receptionist, G=Guest)

R: Hello, operator speaking. May I help you?

G: Hello, this is Mr. Brown in Room 1306. There's been an accident in my room.

R: Oh, dear. What's up?

G: My wife has slipped in the bathroom and sprained her ankle. She can't stand up now.

R: I'm sorry to hear that. Please remain still. I'll send up a first aid worker to help you.

G: Please be quick. Her ankle hurts badly. I think it might be broken.

R: Don't worry. Our fist aid worker is on her way now. I will call an ambulance too.

G: Thanks.

DialogueB-Scripts:

Scene: A guest asks the room attendant to get him some medicine.

(A=Attendant, G=Guest)

A: May I come in? It's the room attendant.

G: Come in please. I'm not feeling good. I've got a terrible stomachache and have loose bowels.

A: I'm sorry to hear that. You really look so pale. Would you like me to call a doctor for you?

G: Not necessary. But could you get some medicine for me?

A: Certainly, sir. I'll do it immediately.
G: Could you please give me some water?
A: Here you are.

Answers:

in Room 1306
an accident
slipped in the bathroom
remain still
a first aid worker
call an ambulance
a terrible stomachache
look so pale
call a doctor
get some medicine
give me some water

Practice: 略

2. Elevator Emergency

Dialogue-Scripts:

Scene: There are some guests stuck in the hotel lift. A guest presses the emergency button for help. After being rescued by the technicians, the guest describes what has happened to her friend.

(S=Staff, G1=Guest1, G2=Guest2)

S: Hello! Is anybody there?
G1: I'm stuck in the lift. Please help.
S: Oh, I'm sorry. On which floor, madam?
G1: Heaven knows! It could be anywhere between 11th to the 12th floor.
S: Calm down, madam. The technicians are on their way. Is there anyone else with you?
G1: Yes, there are 2 other people in the lift.
S: OK. Please do not force the lift door open with your hands, nor try to climb out from the lift. Relax and we'll get you out soon.
G1: OK. Be quick.

…

(The guest has been rescued and meets her friend)

G2: You look a little nervous today.
G1: I feel very anxious. The lift I was in this morning stopped between the 11th and 12th floors!
G2: That sounds terrible. What did you do?

G1: I pressed the emergency button! And then I stayed in the elevator waiting to be rescued.

G2: Was there anyone else with you?

G1: Of course, there were 2 other people in the elevator. We were all scared.

G2: And then what happened?

G1: The technicians came to rescue us. They told us to stay calm and relax, while they tried to fix the problem.

G2: How long did they take to get you out?

G1: Only about 20 minutes, but I was still very nervous.

G2: I would be too!

Answers:

a. It stopped between the 11th and 12th floors.

b. 3 people.

c. They should stay calm and relax.

d. They should not force the lift door open with hands, nor try to climb out from the lift.

e. About 20 minutes.

Practice:

Overloading is prohibited. No slapping. Don't force the door open. No playing or jumping. Don't stand in front of the automatic door. Don't use the elevator when there is a fire. No leaning. Don't push the buttons randomly.

3. Fire Emergency

Dialogue-Scripts:

Scene: When there's a fire emergency in hotel, all of the people there should be informed and instructed how to escape.

1. "Ladies and gentlemen, attention please. The fire alarm has been activated in the building and we are investigating the situation. Please do not panic and listen to the speaker for further instruction. Thank you!"

2. "Ladies and gentlemen, attention please. We have investigated the situation and found it to be a false alarm. We regret any inconvenience caused. Thank you."

3. "Ladies and gentlemen, attention please. There is an emergency situation in the building. Please evacuate by the nearest exit staircase and obey all instructions given by the fire wardens. Do remember to avoid the use of lifts."

4. Ladies and gentleman, attention please! There is a small fire in hotel but it is already under control, so please remain calm. For your safety, please follow me to the lobby using the emergency exit. Please leave your luggage behind and don't use the elevator. Thank you for your cooperation.

5. "Ladies and gentlemen, attention please. The emergency situation in the building is now under control. We regret any inconvenience caused. Thank you."

Answers:

The fire alarm has been activated

Please do not panic

further instruction

have investigated the situation

an emergency situation

obey all instructions

avoid the use of lifts

under control

using the emergency exit

Thank you for your cooperation

regret any inconvenience caused

Practice:

Hazards: Missing/ broken fire safety equipment, Accumulated trash, Open fire doors, Locked exit doors, Blocked stairways, Burned out exit lights.

III. Exercise

Translations:

1. My husband has fainted.
2. I have a terrible tooth-ache, could you buy some medicine for me?
3. Shall I call a doctor for you?
4. We'd better press the emergency button, and then stay in the elevator waiting to be rescued.
5. Please do not worry. This is only a fire drill.
6. 让我在伤口上涂些碘酒。
7. 请冷静，医生马上就来。
8. 我乘坐的电梯在10层与11层之间卡住了。
9. 遇到紧急情况，按照电梯里面的说明去做，并设法让其他人保持冷静。
10. 请遵从消防员的指挥，从最近的疏散通道立即撤离大楼。

Discussion: 略

Draw a line

typhoon—(f)   fire—(c)   heart attack—(e)

loss of property—(a)   elevator accident—(g)   power failure—(d)

tumble—(b)

Scene Two — Settling Complaints

I. Activities

1. Settling Complaints about Reservation

Dialogue-Scripts:

Scene: A guest comes to the hotel to check in, when the receptionist finds the room reserved by the guest has been let to another guest.

(R=Receptionist, C=Customer)

R: Good evening. Welcome to our hotel. What can I do for you?

G: Yes, I have a reservation with you.

R: In whose name was the reservation made?

G: John Smith.

R: Just a moment, please. I'll check the reservation record … Sorry, I'm afraid we have no record of your reservation. When and where was it made?

G: It was made online two days ago from Beijing.

R: Wait a moment, please. I'll check our reservation again … Thank you for waiting, sir. I'm sorry, but the room has been let to somebody else.

G: What! How could you do that to me?

R: Calm down. Look, it's 9 p.m. now. We thought you would not come tonight, because we only hold the room reservation till 6 p.m. It is the hotel policy.

G: You should have called me for confirmation before you let the room to others! Can't you give me another single room?

R: We're awfully sorry, but I'm afraid no single room is available.

G: I reserved the room in advance, but you still have no room for me! I'd never expected such a thing to happen.

R: We do apologize for the inconvenience. Maybe we can offer you a standard room with the same room rate of a single room.

G: If that's the case … alright.

R: Thank you for your understanding.

Answers:

In whose name was the reservation made

check the reservation record

two days ago

let to somebody else

the hotel policy

called me for confirmation

expected such a thing to happen

a standard room

your understanding

Practice:

I'm sorry to hear that.

We are extremely/ terribly sorry for that.

We apologize for the trouble/ mistake/ inconvenience.

We do apologize for that. We will handle it right away.

This is very unusual in our hotel. I will attend to it right now.

2. Settling Complaints about Room Facilities

Dialogue-Scripts:

Scene: A guest just checked in and she is not satisfied with her room. She calls the Front Office, complaining about her room.

(O=Operator, G=Guest)

O: Good evening, Front Office. Can I help you?

G: This is Susan, Room 1503. I've just checked in and I'm not happy with my room.

O: May I know what is wrong?

G: The room is smelly. There is a stain on the sheet and some hairs on the pillow. There are no towels or toilet paper in the bathroom. The television doesn't work. I didn't expect these things would happen in your hotel!

O: I'm terribly sorry to hear that. We have been extremely busy with a large conference. What's more, it's the peak season. We might have overlooked some points.

G: I don't care. I want to change rooms. I can no longer stand being here.

O: I'm sorry for your inconvenience, but I'm afraid there is no vacant room now. Would you mind waiting for about 20 minutes. I'll immediately send a housemaid to make up your room again and a maintenance man to check the television. I promise everything will be in order soon.

G: Do I have any other choice? Well, I'll wait, then.

O: Thanks for your understanding, madam. Would you like to have a drink in our lobby with our compliments?

G: OK. But I hope I can sleep soon.

O: No problem.

Answers:

a. Room 1503.

b. Because the room is smelly. There is a stain on the sheet and some hairs on the pillow. There are no towels or toilet paper in the bathroom. The television doesn't work.

c. The hotel is busy with a large conference.

d. A maintenance man.

e. She will have a drink in the lobby.

Practice:

1. Listen to the guest patiently and show your sympathy towards the incident.
2. Apologize for any inconvenience or trouble caused by the hotel.
3. Search for the effective way to solve the problem as soon as possible.

3. Settling Complaints about Food

Dialogue-Scripts:

Scene: A guest is unsatisfied with the food he ordered and the long waiting time.

(W=Waitress, G=Guest)

G: Hey, excuse me!

W: May I help you, sir?

G: Yes. We've been waiting for twenty minutes, but nothing has been served. The service has been really slow!

W: I'm very sorry, sir. As you can see, it has been a very busy evening. Several large groups came in at the same time as you, and I agree some guests have to wait. I'm going to check your order with our chef.

…

W: We're so sorry to have kept you waiting. Here is your steak, sir. Please enjoy!

G: Oh! What's wrong with you? The steak is over-cooked and too tough. What I want is a medium steak. I think I told the waitress that very clearly when I ordered.

W: We're extremely sorry about it, sir. I think the waitress didn't get your point when taking the order. I'll send it back to the kitchen and get another one for you.

G: Fine. Please do and hurry up!

W: Just a moment, please.

…

(The steak is served again, and the guests have finished all the food on table)

G: Waitress, where's the cappuccino for my wife? Have you forgotten it? You are really inefficient.

W: I really must apologize for the situation. I'll get it right away … Sorry to have kept you waiting. Here's your cappuccino. And to express our regret for the trouble, we can offer you two complimentary desserts and a 30% discount from the meal.

G: Thanks.

Answers:

a. Because it has been a very busy evening. Several large groups are having meal at the same time.

b. Medium.

c. She gets another steak for the guest.

d. Because he has waited for a long time before the cappuccino is served.

e. She offers the guests two complimentary desserts and a 30% discount from the meal.

Practice: 略

III. Exercise

Translations:

1. I'll send up a chambermaid immediately.
2. I'll look into this matter at once.
3. My meal hasn't come yet. Why does it take so long?
4. If you get your luggage ready, we will arrange you to another room.
5. We do apologize for the inconvenience.
6. 抽水马桶堵住了。我一冲水，水就冒出来。
7. 上一位客人很迟才退房，而您要求马上入住，所以服务员没时间来整理。
8. 我们给您带来这么多麻烦，为了表示歉意，特为您提供 9 折/免费花篮。
9. 您把"请勿打扰"的牌子放在把手上了，所以服务员没来整理房间。
10. 非常抱歉，我马上派工程师来。

Role-play: 略

Writing： 略

Part 6 Hotel Management & Orientation 酒店管理与求职

Brainstorm Answers:

people: general manager, sales& marketing director, HR director, F&B director, sales manager, public relation manger, front office manager, executive house keeper, catering manager, F&B manager, entertainment manager, reservations clerk, operator, receptionist, cashier, bellboy, bellman, room maid, laundry worker …

places: Executive Office, Front Office, Housekeeping Department, Food&Beverage Department, Recreation& Entertainment Department, Engineering Department, Security Department, Sales&Marketing Department, Human Resource, Accounting Department, Purchasing Department …

Scene One Hotel Management

I. Activities

1. Promotion

Dialogue-Scripts:

Scene: Mr. Smith, a representative of China Life Insurance Company Ltd. talks with Felix, the Sales Manager of the hotel about group reservations and the terms.

(S= Mr. Smith, F= Felix)

S: Good morning, I'm John Smith from China Life Insurance Company Ltd.

F: Good morning, Mr. Smith. I'm Felix. I'm glad to meet you.

S: Our company wants to host an annual meeting at your hotel From December 28th to 30th. I want to take up some of your time to discuss the reservations for our groups.

F: I'm glad to hear that and we feel honored that you have chosen our hotel. How many people will attend the meeting?

S: It is expected that 2000 people will attend. Could you give us some idea of their price of your rooms?

F: Of course. Here's a copy of our tariff. We have different rates for groups and for FIT and for different periods of the year, that is, the peak season, the mid season and the low season.

S: May I ask if you give preferential rates to groups?

F: Yes. We usually offer 40% discount off for large groups like yours.

S: Can you give us a bigger discount for such a big group? How about 45% discount?

F: Well, I'm not in a position to agree to such a big reduction. I will have to discuss it with our general manager and I will let you know the decision in a couple of days.

S: That's fine. What about your terms regarding payment?

F: We have here a credit application form. When credit arrangements have been made, we will bill you based on your credit limit and you do not have to pay in advance.

S: Do we have to sign some kind of agreement?

F: Yes, we'll send you a copy of agreement. If you agree to the terms, please sign and return a fax copy to us.

S: That's fine.

F: Mr.Smith, we look forward to hosting your guests and hope to cooperate with you for a long time to come.

Answers:

a. A representative of China Life Insurance Company Ltd.

b. A copy of tariff.

c. No, the room rates are different for different periods of the year.

d. Yes, it is.

e. When credit arrangements have been made, the hotel will bill the group based on the credit limit and the group does not have to pay in advance.

Practice:

Keep the existing customers.

Add new customers.

Optimize the spending of each customer.

Maximize efficiency in our service delivery.

2. Interviews & Orientation

Dialogue-Scripts:

Dialogue A:

Scene: Some interviewers are giving an interview to an applicant who applies for the position of Assistant Food & Beverage Manager.

(I=Interviewer, A=Applicant)

I: So let's talk about Assistant Food & Beverage Manager for a bit. What is it that attracts you to the position?

A: Well, I think the position of Assistant Food & Beverage Manager is a bigger challenge to me. The assistant oversees the entire operations in all areas of Food & Beverage, including Bar, Restaurant, Room Service and Conference & Events. I'd like to know the different functions associated with food and beverages, supervising staff and planning various functions inside the restaurant.

I: All right. So … having said that, why do you believe you're a good fit for Assistant Food & Beverage Manager? What values do you think you share with us?

A: I think the most important one is flexibility to respond to a range of different work situations. Besides, I'm positive, organized, good at communication and have 8 years previous Food & Beverage industry experience.

I: Uh-huh.

A: I understand the importance of upholding a brand reputation and value the effort it takes to provide a globally recognized hospitality experience.

I: Well, you're right. We do value the effort to provide a globally recognized hospitality experience and think it's key to our success. But most people have their own personal career goals as well. What are your long-term objectives?

A: Hmm … well, I have a broad outlook. I definitely plan to stay in the hotel industry, serving guests.

I: Okay, do you have any questions about the job?

A: Well, what benefits can I get from the position?

I: The benefits will include a competitive starting salary and holiday entitlement. As an employee you will become a member of the Hilton Club which provides reduced hotel room rates in our hotels worldwide, plus discounts on products and services offered by Hilton Worldwide and its partners. If you get the job, you'll discover many other benefits for yourself.

A: Great. I hope I can get the chance.

I: Well, I think it's time to start wrapping up. George, Cindy, do you have anything to add?

I2: No, I'm good.

I3: I think we're all set.

I: All right. Thanks for coming, Owen. We'll finish reviewing all the candidates in the next couple of days. If you're selected for the position, we'll notify you by email.

A: Thank you, Ms. Li. And thank you too, Ms. Wei and Mr. Zhu, for your time.

Answers:

7→5→1→6→2→4→3

Practice: 略

Dialogue B:

Scene: A new employee reports on his first day of work. The Training Manager is talking to him.

(E= employee, M= Manager)

M: Good morning. Welcome to our hotel. It's your first day of work at our hotel, isn't it?

E: Yes.

M: According to our hotel's regulations, every new employee is required to attend an orientation meeting in the first week.

E: What can I expect to find out?

M: The hotel history and culture, the hotel brand and its properties, the functions of our hotel departments as well as the hotel rules and regulations.

E: Oh, so much information I need to remember!

M: Don't worry. We'll give you a handbook before training which has detailed descriptions in it. You are now a representative of our hotel, so general grooming and standards should be applied during working times.

E: I see. Could you be more specific?

M: OK. You should wear hotel uniforms provided by the hotel during working hours. Have a neat and professional appearance at all times. You should pay attention to your hair, uniform, shoes and nails. Your hair should be above the collar of the shirt. Your uniform must be clean and well-pressed. Shoes should be properly polished. Nails must be well trimmed and clean. And you are not allowed to have a beard.

E: I see.

M: The image of the hotel is reflected by the professionalism of the staff, so you must know our hotel's specialties and services well. Be courteous and cheerful at all time.

E: OK. What else do I need to know?

M: Well, when you come to work, don't bring your personal problems to the work place.

E: Thank you for all your information.

M: You're welcome.

Answers:

hotel's regulations

orientation meeting

the hotel brand

the hotel rules and regulations

a handbook

a representative of our hotel

grooming and standards

hotel uniforms

professional appearance

be clean and well-pressed

have a beard

specialties and services

personal problems

Practice:

a. Pick up the phone gently.

b. Use standard greetings "Good morning/ afternoon/ evening. Identify outlet and yourself. How may I help you?"

c. Use guest's name if known.

d. Listen attentively to guest's needs.

e. Provide guest with appropriate assistance/ information.

f. Thank guest for calling.

III. Exercise

Translations:

1. We'll be advertising the discount on the Internet.

2. Pay for one budget room, and get one free.

3. Why did you leave your last job?

4. Do you work well under pressure?

5. You should keep hotel rules and regulations in mind.

6. 我们对老顾客实施忠诚卡计划。

7. 我过去的经验同这份工作密切相关，我有信心把它做好。因此我很想得到这一职位。

8. 你如何评估自己是位专业人员呢？

9. 你如何处理与同事在工作中的意见不合？

10. 从现在起，你就是我们酒店的代表，有必要注重个人卫生及合理装束。

Role-play: 略

Reading:

(1) asked   (2) company   (3) homework   (4) look   (5) that

(6) guarantee   (7) weakness   (8) why   (9) polished   (10) applying

(11) preparation (12) clearly   (13) normal   (14) interest   (15) information

(16) into

Scene Two — Career and Resume

I. Activities

1. Career Advice

Dialogue-Scripts:

What is the Career Planning Process?

The Career Planning Process includes the stages involved in discovering a career path, including self-assessment, research, decision making, job searching, and accepting a job offer.

Step 1: Self-assessment is a vital and often overlooked step in planning your various career paths. In order to evaluate the suitability of work options, it is important to know who you are as a person. This involves taking a careful inventory of your current career values, interests, skills and personal qualities.

A career counselor can help you with this process through counseling, Exercise and interest/personality inventories.

Once you have articulated a sense of the satisfaction you would like to derive from your work and the skills you have to offer employers, you can begin your research. This stage involves brainstorming possible options and investigating them thoroughly. You will learn about the descriptions of and qualifications for positions, typical entry points and advancement, satisfactions, frustrations, and other important facts in order to determine if there is a good fit.

Step 2: Research — Online resources are available to help you with your preliminary information gathering.

The next step will be to speak with as many people as possible that are involved in work that is of interest to you. By interviewing these individuals for information and advice about their work, you will be getting an insider's perspective about realities of the field and recommended preparation, including graduate study.

Internships and part-time jobs are an excellent way to sample a field of interest. They provide the opportunity to perform some of the job functions, observe others' work and evaluate the environment. Some individuals observe professionals in various fields for a shorter period of time than an internship. These job shadowing experiences, or externships, can last from one morning to several weeks.

Step 3: Decision — making involves an evaluation of the pros and cons for the options you have been researching. It also involves prioritizing and, for some, risk-taking. Since the landscape of the world-of-work is constantly changing, it may be unrealistic to aim for decisions based on absolute certainty.

Adaptability, the ability to manage several options at once, and the ability to maintain a positive attitude when faced with uncertainty may be easy for some while others may find these traits a stretch. Self-awareness, occupational awareness and intuition can all play a part in your decision-making.

Step 4: Search — Once you have identified a work objective, you can begin your job search. Most people will be involved with activities such as networking, identifying prospective employers, writing cover letters and resumes, and interviewing.

Step 5: Acceptance — Finally, you will accept employment. Ideally, it will mark the beginning, or a milestone, in your exciting and varied career. If you are like most Americans, you will change jobs for 8~12 times during your work life. You will continue the process of self-assessment, research and decision-making in order to make effective and fulfilling changes.

Answers:

self-assessment, job searching, career paths, career values, personal qualities, satisfaction, possible options, descriptions of, qualifications, interviewing, information, advice, graduate study, part-time, opportunity, observe, evaluate, Decision-making, risk-taking, unrealistic, positive attitude, play a part in, cover letters, resumes, interviewing, milestone, 8-12 times

Practice:

1. assessments   2. evaluate   3. involve   4. derive from   5. investigating
6. performing   7. risk taking   8. positive

2. Resume Templates

Answers:

a. The applicant's name is Leah Squire. The cell phone number is 123-555-9653.

b. Bachelor of Arts.

c. English.

d. Dining Hall Assistant, Administrative Aide, and Waiter.

e. During summer 2010—summer 2011.

Practice: 略

III. Exercise

Translations:

1. I have received an English education, and have a slight knowledge of Spanish.
2. I have had five years' experience in a company as a salesman.
3. Since my graduation from the school two years ago, I have been employed in Green Hotel as a cashier.
4. I'm highly organized and efficient.
5. I am enclosing a brief resume as you requested. Please let me know if you want an interview.
6. 本人毕业于香港大学，并在加州大学获得文学硕士学位。
7. 我是一名上进心强又可靠的人，并且身体健康，性格开朗。
8. 我善于同各种人员打交道。
9. 我具有良好而广泛的社会关系。
10. 如贵公司有意面试，本人一定遵照所指定的时日前往。

Discussion: 略

Writing: 略

Appendix I
Traditional Festivals　中西方重要传统节日

节日	英文名称	时间
元旦	New Year's Day	1月1日
情人节	Valentine's Day	2月14日
元宵节	Lantern Festival	农历正月十五日
狂欢节（巴西）	Carnival	2月中下旬
桃花节（日本）	Peach Flower Festival	3月3日
国际妇女节	International Women's Day	3月8日
圣帕特里克节（爱尔兰）	St. Patrick's Day	3月17日
枫糖节（加拿大）	Maple Sugar Festival	3—4月
愚人节	Fool's Day	4月1日
复活节	Easter	春分月圆后第一个星期日
宋干节（泰国）	Songkran Festival	泰历新年四月十三日
国际劳动节	International Labor's Day	5月1日
母亲节	Mother's Day	5月的第二个星期日
开斋节	Lesser Bairam	4月或5月（回历十月一日）
国际儿童节	International Children's Day	6月1日
父亲节	Father's Day	6月的第三个星期日
端午节	Dragon Boat Festival	农历五月初五
仲夏节	Mid-Summer Day	北欧6月
古尔邦节（伊斯兰）	Corban	7月下旬
筷子节（日本）	Chopsticks Day	8月4日
中秋节	Mid-Autumn Day	农历八月十五
教师节	Teacher's Day	9月10日
敬老节	Old People's Day	9月15日
啤酒节（德国）	Oktoberfest	9—10月
万圣节	Halloween	10月31日
感恩节	Thanksgiving	11月的最后一个星期四
平安夜	Christmas Eve	12月24日
圣诞节	Christmas Day	12月25日
节礼日	Boxing Day	12月26日
新年除夕	New Year's Eve	农历每年大年三十
春节	Spring Festival	农历大年初一

Appendix II
Housekeeping Vocabulary 客房常用物品

Bathroom 洗手间			
towel 毛巾	face towel 小方巾	bath towel 浴巾	bath mat 地巾
toothbrush 牙刷	toothpaste 牙膏	shampoo 洗发水	conditioner 护发素
shower gel 沐浴露	body lotion 沐浴乳	soap 香皂	comb 梳子
shower cap 浴帽	bath robe 浴袍	shower curtains 浴帘	rubber mat 防滑垫
bath tub 浴缸	tap 水龙头	sewing kit 针线包	hairdryer 吹风机
mug 口杯	mirror 镜子	tissue 面纸	toilet paper 卫生纸

Bedroom 客房			
quilt 被子	blanket 毯子	pillow 枕头	sheet 床单
clothes-hanger 衣架	laundry list 洗衣单	laundry bag 洗衣袋	slippers 拖鞋
iron 熨斗	ironing board 熨衣板	transformer 变压器	adapter 插头
shoes board 鞋拔子	electric kettle 电热水壶	switch board 控制面板	TV remote control 电视遥控器
wall lamp 壁灯	table light 台灯	floor lamp 落地灯	light bulb 电灯泡
safety chain 安全链	lock 门锁	peep hole 门镜猫眼	mini-bar 房内小冰箱
air-conditioner 空调	bathroom scale 体重秤	cup 茶杯	candy bottle 糖果盅
drawer 抽屉	arm chair 扶手椅	telephone 电话	ball pen 圆珠笔

Appendix III
Tableware 餐饮常用物品

Glassware 玻璃器皿			
water glass 水杯	champagne tulip 香槟杯	champagne flute 笛形香槟杯	beer glass 啤酒杯
beer mug 马克杯	brandy snifter 白兰地酒杯	highball glass 高球杯	martini glass 马提尼酒杯
collins glass 柯林杯	red wine glass 红葡萄酒杯	white wine glass 白葡萄酒杯	juice glass 果汁杯
old fashion 古典杯	wine carafe 调酒瓶	water pitcher 水扎	sherry glass 雪莉杯
Silverware 银器			
dinner knife 餐刀	dinner folk 餐叉	fish knife 鱼刀	fish folk 鱼叉
salad knife 沙拉刀	salad folk 沙拉叉	steak knife 牛排刀	butter knife 牛油刀
dessert knife 甜品刀	dessert folk 甜点叉	dessert spoon 甜品勺	cocktail folk 果叉
tea spoon 茶匙	coffee spoon 咖啡匙	table spoon 公匙	soup spoon 汤匙
Chinaware 陶瓷器			
base plate 底碟	round plate 圆碟	oval plate 椭圆碟	dinner plate 餐碟
salad plate 沙拉盘	dessert plate 甜点盘	soup plate 汤盘	sauce dish 调料碟
soup cup 汤盅	soup cup saucer 汤盅垫碟	coffee cup 咖啡杯	coffee cup saucer 咖啡杯垫碟
salt shaker 盐瓶	bowl 碗	cereal bowl 麦片盅	sugar bowl 糖盅
butter dish 黄油碟	tea pot 茶壶	casserole 砂锅	ash-tray 烟灰缸

（续表）

Linen 布草类			
table cloth 台布	table skirt 台裙	table mat 台垫布	tray mat 托盘垫布
over-lay 台布盖布	napkin 餐巾	napkin ring 餐巾环	service cloth 席位巾
hand towel 毛巾	cleaning cloth 擦杯布	leaning towel 抹布	apron 围裙

Appendix IV
Food 食物常用词汇

Fish 鱼类			
salmon 三文鱼	tuna 金枪鱼	cod 鳕鱼	trout 鳟鱼
sea bass 海鲈鱼	sardine 沙丁鱼	abalone 鲍鱼	Halibut 大比目鱼
carp 鲤鱼	anchovy 凤尾鱼	caviar 鱼子酱	role 鱼子
Seafood 海鲜类			
crab 螃蟹	prawn 大虾	langoustine 海螯虾	crayfish 小龙虾
lobster 龙虾	shrimp 虾仁	scallop 扇贝	clam 蛤蜊
oyster 生蚝	mussel 海虹	squid 鱿鱼	octopus 八爪鱼
Dairy 乳制品类			
milk 牛奶	cream 奶油	sour cream 酸奶油	yogurt 酸奶
skim milk 脱脂牛奶	butter milk 黄油牛奶	whole milk 全脂牛奶	cheese 奶酪
Berry 浆果类			
strawberry 草莓	blueberry 蓝莓	blackberry 黑莓	raspberry 覆盆子
cranberry 蔓越莓	mulberry 桑葚	loganberry 罗甘莓	blackcurrant 黑加仑
Vegetable 蔬菜类			
cucumber 黄瓜	eggplant 茄子	carrot 胡萝卜	potato 土豆
celery 芹菜	tomato 番茄	cabbage 卷心菜	bean 豆子
mushroom 蘑菇	onion 洋葱	spinach 菠菜	asparagus 芦笋
olive 橄榄	broccoli 西兰花	avocado 牛油果	lettuce 生菜
cauliflower 菜花	sweet potato 红薯	pepper 辣椒	kale 羽衣甘蓝

参 考 文 献

[1] 袁露，阮蓓，李飞. 酒店英语[M]. 天津: 天津大学出版社，2010.
[2] Practical English For U.S. Restaurant, Times Publishing (NY)ltd.
[3] 胡扬政. 现代酒店服务英语[M]. 北京：清华大学出版社，2013.
[4] 胡扬政. 酒店英语服务实训[M]. 北京：清华大学出版社，2010.
[5] 郭兆康. 饭店情景英语[M]. 上海：复旦大学出版社，2000.
[6] 王艳,胡新莲. 酒店英语[M]. 重庆：重庆大学出版社,2010.
[7] 王迎新. 酒店英语[M]. 北京：中国林业大学出版社, 2011.
[8] 王艳，任虹. 酒店英语实训教程[M]. 北京：机械工业出版社，2013.
[9] 蔡丽巍. 酒店岗位英语[M]. 北京：国防工业出版社，2012.
[10] 魏新民，申延子. 酒店情景英语[M]. 北京：北京大学出版社, 2011.
[11] 朱华. 酒店英语：视听版[M]. 北京：北京大学出版社，2014.
[12] 江波，李啟金. 酒店实用英语[M]. 天津：天津大学出版社，2011.
[13] Stott, Trish. Highly recommended : English for the hotel and catering industry[M]. Oxford : Oxford University Press, 1994.
[14] Francis O Hara. Be my guest : English for the hotel industry[M]. Cambridge : Cambridge University Press, 2008.
[15] Seymour, Mike. Hotel & hospitality English[M]. London : Collins, 2011.
[16] Talalla, Renee. Main course : language and skills for restaurant workers[M]. Selangor Malaysia: Falcon Press, 2000.
[17] Harding, Keith. High season : English for the hotel and tourist industry[M]. Oxford: Oxford University Press, 1994.

参考网站

http://www.ehow.com/how_4963436_hotel-bed-making-procedures.html.
http://luxurytravel.about.com/od/hotelandresorts/tp/Five-Star-Hotels-Great-Hospitality-Service.htm.
http://www.ehow.com/how_2058263_sell-product.html.
http://www.wikihow.com/Escape-a-Stranded-Elevator.
http://www.wikihow.com/Deal-With-Customer-Complaints.

推荐阅读

"十三五"职业教育国家规划教材
高职高专旅游类专业精品教材

《酒店实用英语(灵活运用篇)》

《酒店实用英语(灵活运用篇)》适合酒店英语中级学习者,旨在培养酒店、旅游管理专业学生和酒店服务人员的英语听说能力及其在实际工作岗位中的英语运用能力,突出行业外语的应用能力培养。该教材还原了酒店工作的本来面貌,注重以实际工作流程为导向,配有课件和音频二维码,同时紧扣《江苏省旅游饭店职业英语等级标准(中级)》,与职业资格证书挂钩、与行业接轨,实现分层次培养人才的目的。本书还密切结合酒店前厅、客房和餐饮等岗位群的典型工作任务,着眼于培养兼具英语语言表达能力、人际交往与沟通协调能力及应变能力综合素质的现代旅游服务业从业人员。

《酒店实用英语(基础会话篇)》

《酒店实用英语(基础会话篇)》适合酒店英语初级学习者。本系列教材内容体系以实际工作流程为导向,让学生自然融入真实情境中,实现掌握职业英语的目的。本书紧扣《江苏省旅游饭店职业英语等级标准(初级)》,共有6个模块、20个主题情境和60个子任务;课文学习内容以完成任务、解决问题入手,侧重听说训练及课堂小组讨论,配有课件和音频二维码,体现职业性、实用性、趣味性和时代感。本套教材既适合高职高专酒店管理专业学生使用,也可作为酒店行业一线员工培训教材和自学读本。